DAVID ROSS

AWESOME
BUSINESS

AWESOME
LIFE

**AN AMBITIOUS BUSINESS OWNERS' GUIDE TO
CONTROLLED, CONSISTENT AND RAPID GROWTH**

This book is dedicated to my father,
who instilled in me, from a very young age,
an appreciation for the written word and
the importance of learning and education.

First published in 2022 by David Ross

A catalogue entry for this book is available from the National Library of Australia.

ISBN: 978-1-922764-00-3

Printed in Australia by McPherson's Printing Group
Book production and text design by Publish Central
Cover design by Pipeline Design

The paper this book is printed on is certified as environmentally friendly.

Disclaimer

CONTENTS

INTRODUCTION

I ask a lot of questions. Here's one for you: have you achieved the things you originally set out to do when you went into business?

It's all too easy to get caught up along the way with the white noise and chaos that creeps in. As a Chartered Accountant and business coach, I regularly see business owners end up totally frustrated and gassed, with each year just rolling by. I also see successful businesses stall, struggle to get to the next level or, at times, go backwards. The owners of these businesses deal with an endless tussle between their business lives and their personal lives, often destroying one or both in the process.

The common thread that unites these business owners is that they lack a structured approach to achieving their business outcomes. Instead, their business becomes reactive and ad hoc, and ends up off course.

The issue isn't that your business is on its last legs… it's probably far from it. It might simply be that you haven't implemented structure around what you want or how to get there. The drive and resources are there, but the guidance needed to achieve the results isn't.

I have always believed in the impact a great advisor can have on a business. It is unfortunate that we live in a world where many think the answers can be found at the end of a Google search. Business owners who take this route typically end up down an endless rabbit hole of information, only to wake up one day and realise they have implemented and achieved very little.

Since 2001, I have worked with more than 1200 small business owners just like you. Being a Chartered Accountant with the nuanced skills of business coaching seemed a natural integration to me. The inability of both coaches and accountants to embrace both skill sets still surprises me.

When I started my accounting firm two decades ago, I did so with the purpose of working with business owners on much more than just tax. After all, tax is just a by-product of having a successful business. If you aren't making money, you don't have a tax problem.

Starting a business from scratch, though, meant that I had to take on clients that possibly weren't a great fit. I sold a share of my business to a colleague, and we quickly grew to the stage where we both offered an interest to a third accountant. Fast forward a number of years and we found ourselves with 15 staff, two offices, seven-figure revenue and great clients.

But something was missing.

The business had become everything I *didn't* want. The work wasn't satisfying and the business was heading in a totally different direction to what I originally intended.

After buying out one of the directors, the remaining owner and I decided to split our two offices into separate firms.

It was time for a new plan – to take a step back from the traditional tax firm and reset. It was time to focus on what I originally set out to do when I went into business: provide business clients with not only key advice around the numbers, but also strategy and operations.

This led me to develop key skills in neuro-linguistic programming (NLP) and mental health first aid; take on speaking and panellist gigs at industry events; and start hosting a podcast. Through all of this came the key understanding that success is not just about the numbers – it's also about the human emotion behind business decisions, and how powerfully it can affect our working and personal lives.

TAKING A STRUCTURED APPROACH

My aim in this book is to take my vast knowledge and experience and provide you with five key disciplines that, when mastered and applied consistently, will see your business achieve rapid, sustainable growth and have a massive impact on your life.

As a small business owner you probably face three main issues:

1. **Financial dissatisfaction:** You are frustrated with your lack of progress and don't have a good grasp on the financial side of your business. You have probably scratched your head in wonder: *where did the years go?* There is also often a compounding effect when finances go unchecked year after year.
2. **Overwhelm:** You feel disorganised and inefficient, and never have enough time to do it all. This typically leads to increased stress and often health or relationship issues. Maybe you miss out on life's moments because you are always 'flat out'.
3. **Lack of focus or a clear plan:** Everything is kept in your head. This means you're always changing things, every time a new, bright, shiny object comes along. Your business never gets a chance to grow. It's two steps forward and three steps back.

If you're like most small business owners, your business is your second-largest asset beyond your home. Failure to grow the value of your business consistently results in poor wealth creation, and the feeling of things just not getting anywhere.

Look, I get it: business can be tough. It can be complicated. Most of all, it can be a lonely journey.

However, having a structured approach to managing your business provides clarity and focus to address the three main issues you're facing. It allows you to implement actions and deal with ad-hoc issues as they arise, in an orderly fashion.

The approach I outline in this book will help you understand where you are now, where you are going and how you are going to get there. Then it's a case of consistent improvement and accountability.

THE VECTOR BUSINESS PLATFORM: DIRECTION AND MAGNITUDE

In science, a vector is a measurement that has both a direction and a magnitude. Similarly, to create an awesome business and awesome life, you need to know where you are going (direction) and create the results you need to get there (magnitude).

In the following chapters, I will introduce you to a structured approach called the Vector Business Platform. The Vector Business Platform enables you to achieve your outcomes through a proven five-step process:

1. Awareness
2. Numbers
3. Planning
4. Improvement
5. Accountability.

As a Vector Business, you will move through continuous 12-month cycles of development. As one plan ends, another begins – this time from a more advanced starting point. As your business evolves, so does your life. They go hand in hand.

Why is the Vector Business Platform so successful? Well, conventional accountants are focused on compliance and look to the past. Conventional coaches look towards the future; but as a whole, they lack substance, and have a poor understanding of business financials. Conventional accountants will talk to you about tax, with any help in achieving business growth and success a mere afterthought. Conventional coaches say, 'Here, buy my over-hyped program!' (online gurus) or, 'Here, use this procedure I've created for you!' (consultants).

The Vector Business Platform combines the strengths of each approach and overcomes the weaknesses to create a far more holistic method for evolving businesses. Becoming a Vector Business is about evolving your business beyond the conventional boundaries of business advice to an integrated platform. It means less hype and more substance, always with a keen eye on the financial aspects.

Instead of ignoring the impact that your business and personal lives have on each other, the Vector Business Platform supports you to achieve the very things that you originally set out to do, by shifting your focus to your needs.

By following the concepts in *Awesome Business Awesome Life*, you will achieve more direction with more speed and more impact in both your business and personal lives.

It's time we rolled up our sleeves and got to work, don't you think?

PART I
DEPARTURES

Business is a journey. You depart from where you are now and take flight towards your destination, with the view to arriving in great shape at the other end. This section is about readying you for your journey, ensuring all crosschecks are done. Time to check in.

CHAPTER 1

THE YIN AND THE YANG OF IT

Business owners often list 'freedom' as a key reason for taking the big step. It could be freedom from working for that boss you couldn't stand. It could be freedom from doing unsatisfying work in your job. It could even be freedom away from your spouse – having an individual outlet for your energies or talent.

It intrigues me, then, that so much has been written about work/life balance. If being in business was designed to provide freedom, why do we need balance? Balance from what? Clearly, business doesn't provide what we seek all the time. In fact, once you get past the excitement of startup phase, business is often seen as the dark side. Personal life, which takes a back seat for a while, represents the light. It becomes what commands our desire.

This interaction is at the core of any attempt to improve your world. You can't have a great business without tending to it with significant hours, yet you can't have a great personal life without keeping focus on it. Neglect one or the other and you will struggle.

YOUR BUSINESS LIFE

While you may have altruistic reasons for being in business, your ultimate aim should be to generate a profit. Even if you are a not for profit or member-based organisation, your aim is to maximise your results for key stakeholders. The fact is, you cannot do anything in your business life unless you have money. No level of impact can be made without available funds.

Using this, then, as our basic premise for a small business, your aim as the owner should be to create profit, surplus cashflow and growth towards your ultimate goals.

Simple, huh?

Maybe not. Australian Government statistics show that only 65% of businesses survive past their fourth year. Clearly, business success takes focused effort, great management and, at times, slices of luck. Unfortunately there is often a badge of honour that is worn when it comes to the number of hours a small business owner works.

It is a strange scenario that freedom is one of the core reasons many people go into business, yet once in business you find yourself chained to the work – a slave to the very freedom machine you wanted to create. Long hours and wearing the hat for every different role within the business tends to lead to burnout or disinterest in what once fuelled your passion. The fulfilment and purpose that once drove you disappears.

Recognising this phenomenon is essential to gaining control over your business. Hard work does not necessarily equal better results. Yet not working at all can have a massive impact. I have seen many business owners get so dialled in to the whole working ON your business concept that they move away too soon.

Until the business is properly cooked – running smoothly with systems and procedures in place, and able to sustain additional team members who can adequately fulfil the owner's role – moving on can mean disaster.

YOUR PERSONAL LIFE

What makes a great personal life? Every individual has different values and priorities. Some find great importance in spirituality; others focus on health and wellbeing. For many it is the impact of family and friends that matters. For bigger-picture people it may be the legacy you will leave behind. This great melting pot of life has so many facets that can lead to a person's happiness and fulfilment. It is interesting, then, that the most commonly pitched ideal is that of freedom, or the need to not work.

Don't get me wrong, I'd love to be lying on a beach while I am writing this; however, there are times when you just need to put your head down and get it done.

No matter what your personal drive is, if you own a business, it is the enabler for your personal life. That's your business's job. The business is the money generator, and that's why I think it is seen as the dark in the yin and yang. Personal life is where your good is done; it's where your soul lives. It's the things that you will be. It's where you leave your legacy. You don't leave your legacy as a business. A business can disappear and die just as easily as an individual can disappear and die. However, an individual will be remembered long beyond the typical small business. Businesses will fade; the people who ran them will be what is remembered.

MANAGING THE MIX

The interaction between your business and personal life is more than work/life balance. I like to think of it as what you do with the mix. In the music industry there's the concept of getting the correct mix. As a musician, your mix could be different in any particular venue or room that you play in. The dials all need to be tuned into a different frequency and set at different volumes, otherwise you end up with feedback or a mix that sounds terrible. All of the inputs need to be balanced correctly. It's impossible to have a perfect balance between life and business because sometimes the mix needs to change, depending on the environment – just like how the music mix needs to change depending on the dynamics of any particular room.

Let's look at some of the reasons why the mix may need to change so you can align your personal life with your business life at any point in time.

Quite often, a recalibration is required if you're going through some sort of turmoil in your personal life. Your business starts to suffer because you must (rightly) focus your attention on your personal turmoil rather than your business. There are some people who may just launch themselves doubly into their business during times of turmoil – they'll double down and just go at it regardless. I once participated in an interview with a business owner and a union representative over an employee dispute. During the interview, the union representative received a phone call to say that his wife had been in a car accident. He took the call, gave a message to the caller, and then went straight on with the meeting. It was the steely resolve that he continued with that was confronting to watch. It was a great example of when the balance goes too far one way.

Personal turmoil comes in many forms, however its impact needs to be closely managed.

When a business is underperforming, those stresses infiltrate into your personal life. The effect of poor business performance on personal money worries is one of the biggest issues in relationships. When this happens, the personal turmoil resulting from arguments and self-isolation then loop back to causing business underperformance. It becomes a self-defeating cycle. This is where you've got to get the mix right.

If you are significantly overworked in your business, you may need to build in more leisure time.

It might also be exactly the opposite. Maybe you've put too much leisure into the mix and you actually need to concentrate on the actions required to get your business to a level where it's financially able to employ more people – eventually allowing you to pull back a bit and give more attention to life.

At any one point in time, you have to adjust the mix, depending on the environment. Understanding the interplay between business life and personal life is the only resolution that you can make. You need to realise when you need to change the mix. You need to understand what the different mixes are at any point in time and the stresses that may occur, both on a personal and a business level.

Not getting it right means you will simply go around in circles. You will work too many hours, then realise you need to delegate. You can't afford to delegate, so you need to earn more in your business. You can't earn more, so you need to improve your business, and to improve your business, you decide to work harder.

The cycle continues, and your personal life continues to suffer.

Without the right mix, everything becomes slightly off tilt. Your business suffers, or your relationships, health and time with family suffer.

So, what can I recommend to help you deal with this mix and make sure you get this interplay right?

Working on the mix is the key, and to do that you need a plan and a way to achieve it.

DIRECTION, SPEED, IMPACT

As shown in figure 1.1, the Awesome Business Awesome Life model is centred around your personal and business lives. It is important to surround the core with a number of layers, each critical for implementation and achieving sustainable results.

Figure 1.1: Overview of the Awesome Business
Awesome Life Model

The first of these surrounding layers provides structure and focus. By putting in place a structured method of business improvement you will achieve three things:

1. **Direction:** Clarity on where your business is going.
2. **Speed:** With a clear plan and laser focus, you will achieve results faster than meandering by yourself as the business calendar ticks over year after year.
3. **Impact:** Achieving the things you set out to do in business will allow you to make a far greater impact, whether that be to your own life or to others. You can't make impact until your business and life enables you to.

CREATE, IMPLEMENT, ACHIEVE

To manage the interaction between your business and personal life it is essential to check in with what you want to achieve and how you are going to get there. Many great businesses have failed due to business owners not achieving what they envisaged. The art of implementation is key to progress and ultimate achievement.

Great businesses are constantly evolving. Evolving, however, should not be mistaken for unplanned change. To be successful in both your business and personal life you need to control the process. You are creating your vision, not someone else's. Unfortunately, for many business owners this does not occur beyond opening day.

As your business's creator, have you contemplated what your business will look like once it has reached its destination? Once you arrive, what then?

I want you to take a few minutes and answer the following questions:

- In what year in the future do you want your business to be complete, operating 100% to your satisfaction, financially and personally?
- At that point:
  - What sales revenue/income are you earning?
  - How much are you personally taking as a wage/ dividend/drawing?
  - How many staff do you have?
  - What BIG things are happening in your personal life?

How did you go? This is a very big-picture exercise I know. We will cover detailed planning in Chapter 6, but for now, I just want you to take a look at what you wrote. Do you feel it is achievable? Did you go the easy route, or did you stretch yourself? Remember this is YOUR business and YOUR life. If you are not creating what you want, who are you working for?

Now here's the biggest thing that will move you from your sheet of paper to achieving what you set out to do. It's implementation. As Thomas Edison is quoted as saying: 'Vision without execution is just hallucination.'

Now, I know when you wrote down the answers to this exercise you were having doubts. You probably thought, *I can't get all of this done.* You may have written down less than you could actually achieve because of that little niggling voice in the back of your head. It's time to call that little voice out. You can achieve whatever you want – you just need structure.

Implementation is critical to the success of any plan. If you have a realistic plan and implement the strategies required, you will leave no stone unturned in your effort to achieve your target. Monitoring and improvement of those strategies is likely to be required to achieve the success you desire, but unless you implement your strategies, you won't get anywhere near improving. Instead, you will stand still, and in this fast-paced business world, you will be run over.

For great implementation to occur you need to follow four steps:

1. **Define clear objectives and strategies:** Formulate specific and measurable objectives ('the what'), along with key strategies ('the how'), as part of your overall plan.
2. **Set specific actions:** Each strategy needs detailed to-do items to make sure things happen. These actions will form part of keeping everyone accountable.
3. **Allocate team members to actions and assign deadlines:** There is no point having a big to-do list without any due dates or team responsibility allocated.
4. **Create accountability structure:** Manage points two and three by regularly checking in with a key advisor or team member using a structured accountability agenda.

Creating your overall vision and instilling a culture of implementation allows you to set about achieving results. This is typically where massive improvement will happen in your business. It's your reflection on the outcomes of your implementation that drives this: what worked, what didn't and what needs adjusting.

By having a coach work with you throughout the year, you can build a structure around your business for providing input and feedback on key decisions, as well as drive accountability.

If you stretched yourself when making your notes in the creation exercise earlier, you will most likely agree that there is a hell of a lot of work to be done before you sit here crowing about having achieved it all. There will be laughs, tears, struggles and victories along the way. Remember to celebrate the small wins as these will give you the confidence to keep at it.

Case Study: Starting With a Blank Slate

Michael and Peter are a father and son duo who run a building supplies store. With their store having been established for many years, they have become accustomed to the daily grind – opening the door every morning and taking whatever is thrown their way. It's a successful business, yet when I started working with them they had no real awareness of where their business was or where they wanted to take it, other than to fix their immediate needs – in their case, cashflow. The solution to their cashflow issues was obvious to me; but until THEY became aware of how all the contributors to cashflow were integrated, and the bigger picture required to really get results, they just would not buy in to the ideas I raised. To see the solution, they had to understand concepts like inventory days and how this integrates with shop layout. They had to be across strategies like online design and matching as opposed to stocking every particular variant of a product.

Quite often a business owner is resistant to ideas, dismissively deciding 'that will never work, we've tried that already.' In Michael and Peter's case, they needed a much broader plan to focus on – something larger than their past experience. Add to this some basic business financial literacy and I now have them applying themselves not only to their plan, but also to the cashflow ideas they originally dismissed.

SUMMARY

I'm calling it: there is no such thing as work/life balance. Instead, there is an interaction between your business life and your personal life. At times, the mix will need to be adjusted according to your environment and the situations you find yourself in at any point in time. Always living 100% in either your business or personal life doesn't work. Neither does splitting it perfectly down the middle.

The things that happen in your personal life have a direct impact on your business. When something occurs in your business, there is an impact personally. A constant adjustment of attention between the two is critical to avoid burnout in either world.

To have a truly awesome business and awesome life, you need to start by creating your big picture and then condensing it into a meaningful plan. The hard work then comes by focusing on implementing the plan.

During implementation, you will work to continuously improve, ideally guided and held accountable by a coach with a structured and focused system. This structure and focus provides you with clear direction, increased speed in achieving results, and far greater impact on your own and others' lives. The create, implement and achieve layer surrounds the yin/yang of your business and personal lives, complemented by the outer layer comprising the five components of the Vector Business Platform, starting the process of taking you from where you are now to where you want to be.

CHAPTER 2

WHAT IS A VECTOR BUSINESS?

There are two really important things when it comes to building a successful small business. The first of these is the dollars. Without enough money flowing through a small business's veins, it will fail. Maybe not straight away, but eventually. The second is the path the business takes. Certainty is important – not only of the direction, but also of the actions required to get it where you want to go.

It is not enough to just have dollars in a business. Money is pointless without any sense of forward motion. There is no purpose, very little fulfilment and the very real possibility that at some point, the dollars will just evaporate.

Likewise, it is not enough to simply be clear on where you are going – without the dollars, you will not be able to adequately seize any opportunities presented.

Magic happens when you combine something of magnitude – in a business's case, the dollars – with a direction (or clear plan and actions). In science this is called a vector – a measurement that exhibits both magnitude and direction. The stronger each of these components are, the greater the impact or result.

Think of archery as an example. If you have perfect aim but do not pull the bow back far enough, you will not hit the target. Have perfect tension in the bow yet no idea where you are aiming? You guessed right – time to duck for cover.

A Vector Business is one that understands this combination. Magnitude with direction. Profitability combined with a clear plan and strategy.

WHAT IT'S LIKE NOW

To really progress anything in life, you need to understand what is happening now. This flag in the sand is essential for a number of reasons.

Firstly, there needs to be a base reference point. What is your current financial position – both business and personal? What is your current business value? In which areas are you possibly underperforming?

It's your starting position. To use the flight analogy, this is your departure point. If you don't know where you are, or plan where you are heading, you are not going anywhere.

At the departure point, most businesses experience common issues, no matter what their maturity level. I touched on these three issues in the Introduction, but let's look at them in a bit more detail.

The first of these centres around having a good grasp on financials, so you can avoid financial dissatisfaction.

Understanding how to analyse the financial side of your business is a learned skill. Unfortunately, it is not a mandatory skill when starting a business and, as such, is often an afterthought, with many business owners relying on their key advisors to provide the narrative on the numbers. Now, I'm not saying you need to be an expert in the numbers; however, how much more valuable advice would you get from your advisors if you were talking on equal terms? If those conversations were based around what to do with the information rather than explaining the information, you would see a massive change in the way you work with your accountant or coach.

If you already have a good grasp of the numbers, congratulations. This then brings your next challenge: being able to adequately control the numbers. I'm not talking about poor financial situations here. Let's make the assumption that your business is solvent, albeit underperforming. While you may understand the financials enough to analyse that a problem exists, being able to troubleshoot and come up with strategies around the numbers is key. Inability to master both the knowledge of the numbers and how to positively influence them leads to feeling anxious about your financial security. This anxiety leads to money stress, and subsequently impacts your personal life.

The second area of concern when looking at where you are now is the feeling of overwhelm or disorganisation.

When you first started your business you probably experienced a phase of unbridled enthusiasm as you saw everything come to life – your dream work taking shape and new customers and clients coming on board to get to know. You may have added team members, become involved in community engagement and maybe even won some accolades along the way. As you moved beyond the honeymoon phase, though, the growing pains may have started to kick in. Maybe customer and client demands increased, managing a team turned out to be more difficult than you imagined, and there never seemed to be enough hours in the day to get everything done – let alone have a family life.

So you worked harder. You tried your hand at creating systems; you started to delve into the 'working ON your business' mentality. However, that all reduced the time you spent doing the work, so the jobs piled up, and the cycle seemed never-ending.

This overwhelm is common and comes largely from not having a good grasp on designing your growth phases. There are always going to be times of overwhelm – it's business – and that is at the heart of the yin/yang concept I spoke about in Chapter 1. However, crippling overwhelm can bring a business, and its owner, to its knees.

The third most common issue I encounter is small business owners not having a clear plan of where they are heading. Over 90% of business owners who complete our Vector Business Scorecard and Prioritize needs analysis rank having a business plan as highly important – yet do not have one in place.

A plan is crucial in identifying what you are aiming for (your objective). A great plan also then details how you are going to get there (your strategies). This is then broken down into the specific actions required to make it all happen.

Imagine you decide to go on holiday. Where are you now? Where do you want to go? Once this basic information is researched, you need to determine how you will get there, what modes of transport are required and where you will stay.

Imagine setting off on a holiday with none of this laid out. Sure, it can be done, and some people actually prefer that freewheeling approach; however, by far the more organised and successful way of taking that trip is to plan.

The most common pushback I get when I talk to business owners about planning is that a plan for a business can be made redundant quickly if it is outperformed or something drastic happens.

The other is that it is just as easy to keep the plan in your head rather than spelling it out on paper.

I will bust both of these planning myths a little later on in this book.

Awesome planning is at the heart of awesome businesses.

If you don't have a plan, your business is reactive to everything that happens around it. Decision-making is extremely short term. Results become thrust upon you, rather than you being driven to achieve your goals.

Little wonder no progress occurs, and you spend endless years just watching the world go by.

Case Study: Three Very Different Businesses with Three Very Different Problems

Tony runs a retail heating store. When I met him, he had a wealth of knowledge of his product, but very little idea of how the numbers worked in his business. Gross profit margin was a mystery, as was having a good handle on his business cashflow. Not understanding these issues meant that Tony was constantly worried about when the next supplier bill was due. Money stress at work spilled over into his personal life as well.

Lee is a signwriter. When I met Lee, he was starting work at some ungodly hour, eating meals on the fly and living more hours at work than he was at home with his family. I asked Lee, 'Why the long hours?' His answer was that he needed to work that hard to get all the work done. Turns out, Lee was taking on everything that raised its head. Small jobs, large jobs. Customer asked, Lee said yes. He was overwhelmed, overworked and underpaid.

Stacy is a graphic designer, and a smart one. The problem for Stacy was that she had plenty of ideas and visions, but they were all just spinning around – none implemented or completed. The ideas were not part of where she wanted to take the business – just efforts to grow her revenue. She had no plan, so she was just flitting from one thing to another.

We will see how each of them is doing shortly.

You will get a chance soon to check in with where you are at now in your business. For now, though, let's look at an overview of how a structured process can help address some of your business issues.

THE VECTOR BUSINESS PLATFORM™

Having a structured approach to developing your business removes ad-hoc decisions and the ability to be distracted from the things you are wanting to achieve. For many business owners, managing a business becomes a jigsaw, and at times it has missing pieces.

The first advisor most business owners engage is an accountant; however, accountants are normally used solely to do the following:

- Set up structure and registrations
- Prepare tax and historical financials
- Respond to ad-hoc questions on bookwork.

Accountants are very undervalued and underutilised. A great accountant can provide you with robust business advice based on years of working with thousands of business owners just like you.

A business owner then makes a choice about how they will manage their books. Will they do the bookwork themselves or hire a bookkeeper (internal or external)? Preparing the bookwork yourself can be a time-consuming task, and in some cases cost more than engaging a professional – especially when it comes to managing payroll and staff entitlements.

In fact, this is the case with any professional services for business owners. Trying to perform an internet search to find a solution or template is fraught with danger. Not only will the end result be sub-par, in some cases costing big dollars, the implementation and accountability also suffers.

Take business coaching, for example. There is enough content online for business owners to fill the Grand Canyon, yet without having a professional coach with significant business experience guiding you and assessing your needs, you are likely to struggle to analyse exactly the right solution and fall short in the interpretation and implementation phase.

Sometimes business owners decide to go it alone. This is especially the case when finances are good. I call this business apathy. Typically, this occurs when the business provides a good income, a good lifestyle and a good family setup such as children being in good schools. When life is good, it's human nature that we get comfortable. When we get comfortable, we take our eye off the ball. When this happens, competition starts biting and hopefully, before it's too late, we wake from our slumber to scramble to make changes. Often it becomes everybody else's problem rather than ours. I also see business apathy when it comes time for a business to sell, with owners realising too late that they should have been designing their business for ultimate exit all along.

The way to ensure you make the right choices with your business is to apply a structured approach, and cycle through it on an annual basis. We call this structure the Vector Business Platform (see figure 2.1). It allows you to *create*, *implement* and *achieve* the things you need to create an awesome business and awesome life.

Figure 2.1: The Vector Business Platform

The Vector Business Platform consists of five key disciplines:

1. **Awareness:** Understanding where you are now, what requires focus and what is actually possible.
2. **Numbers:** Gaining control over quality, efficiency and your knowledge of the key financial aspects of your business.
3. **Planning:** Building a solid action plan, getting your team on board and chunking it down to manageable action periods or sprints.
4. **Improvement:** Designing and crafting your business systems and processes by learning what works and what doesn't and adjusting where needed.
5. **Accountability:** Creating at-a-glance management processes and an accountability framework to ensure what should get done actually does.

You work on these five disciplines over 12-month cycles. At the end of the 12 months you return to the start and set plans for the next cycle. It is a much more thorough approach to working with your advisors than, for example, checking in with your accountant once a year, often six to 12 months after the year has actually ended. It provides you with focus and accountability to ensure you're driving results, yet you're also supported by your key advisors or accountability partner. We will cover the specific details of each of the five disciplines in Part II, but for now let's look at why each of the five is critical to your success.

Awareness

American author Tony Alessandra stated, 'Prescription before diagnosis is malpractice.' He was referring to sales, but this equally applies to developing your business. Many business programs are structured in such a way that you learn a few things you need to know and a whole lot you don't. Without truly understanding your business needs, a textbook advisor is only focused on themselves, not on you. Awareness moves that focus and aims the spotlight purely on you. Structured content is not the issue – it is how that content can be used flexibly in your circumstances.

In the Vector Business Platform, the Awareness discipline is designed to help you understand your needs, get a base read on your business value and look for some early wins and profit improvement through hidden profits analysis.

Numbers

Every business owner needs a firm grasp on their numbers. I'm amazed by how many business owners I encounter flying blind, with every financial facet of their business run by the amount of money in their bank account. As part of the Numbers discipline, you'll gain a greater knowledge and appreciation of what your financials mean and how they can be used to make key decisions. It is critical that you stay on top of your financials and tax obligations, including the critical area of tax planning. To round out your mastery of the numbers in your business, it is essential to review your bookwork including the automation of key tasks and processes.

Planning

This discipline is all about getting the plan out of your head and into action. The core of a great plan is setting objectives, solid realistic strategies and the actions that underpin them. It simply isn't possible to achieve an awesome business or awesome life without a clear idea of where your business is heading.

Once your plan is set, it is then best practice to chunk things down into 90-day sprints and involve your team. The team around you is key to implementation and achieving the targets you set. You simply can't do it all. Part of the planning process the Vector Business Platform will take you through is allocating tasks and milestones to key individuals.

It is important to plan not only your business affairs, but also how to protect your assets and wealth. The Planning discipline provides guidelines around how to approach this.

Improvement

Improvement and the subsequent discipline of Accountability work in tandem. Both areas are best approached by partnering with a business coach to ensure maximum results.

Improvement is all about reviewing what works and what doesn't and adjusting accordingly. Systems and procedures are normally the starting point, ensuring that the business runs to a set way of operations.

As you identify areas of improvement, you'll often need extra knowledge and support – particularly around automation and cloud apps.

You'll amplify your impact by applying a monthly check-in rhythm with your key advisor.

Accountability

Nothing happens if you don't do what you say you are going to do. Self-accountability is tough. The skill set required to run the business day in and day out, as well as hold yourself accountable, is complex. It is far too easy to let things slip, and the further you get behind, the harder it becomes to achieve your plan. If you want to create an awesome business, get an accountability partner. Again, by applying a monthly rhythm, you can ensure that you check in with your key financials, monitor a well-designed key performance indicator (KPI) dashboard for at-a-glance metrics, and get the occasional reality check when you are dragging the chain. Often change is a struggle, so having an advisor with key mindset skills is advantageous.

WHERE YOU'D RATHER BE

Now of course there is no point in knowing where you are now, and having a structured approach to make progress, if you have no idea of where you want to be.

In Chapter 6, you will learn how to formulate your plan – but now is the perfect time to think broadly about where you want to be.

To do this properly you need to enter what I call the dream room. A business should be built for your purpose. The magic happens when you are operating according to that purpose. This is where you will truly achieve.

Being realistic does not mean that you cannot dream. A dream gives you the drive and passion to pursue that which consumes you. There is plenty of chance to back it up strongly with numbers as you flesh out the full plan.

So, let's dream a little about your destination.

What will this business of yours look like when it's fully cooked? What will it look like financially? What work will you be doing and who will you be doing it with? What will your life look like? Remember, you may have multiple points in your journey where you ask yourself these questions again. This is because the structured approach may have you either achieving the things that you originally set out to achieve and then asking, *What now?* Or, as you develop as a business, you may decide to change tack and explore a completely different set of end goals.

Remember: it's all about you. It's where YOU would rather be, compared to where YOU are now.

Typically, I see small business owners seeking more time to enjoy life. They want to feel that they have achieved their target and can now pull back a little. This is a great dream but one that should be met with great caution. Pulling away from your business before it is ready is a common mistake. It's natural to want to move towards pleasure and freedom, but do this too soon and you'll risk your business going backwards or stalling. The key is designing the business with complete certainty of where you want it to be and by when.

So, what are you going to head towards? Let's look at some common targets.

Financial Security

Moving towards understanding your business numbers and performance removes a massive amount of stress. We all seek security for our and our family's future, and if you own a business, it all starts here.

The term 'financial security' can mean different things to different people. It can mean consistent cashflow, removing the pressure of chasing your bank balance constantly. It can also mean wealth creation: building assets for the future such as property or financial investments, all enabled by a profitable business.

Financial security, no matter what form it takes, must always start with understanding the numbers. This enables you to make key decisions, take corrective action if necessary and act on opportunities when they arise. Business financial literacy is often an afterthought for business owners – it's often considered the domain of the accountant or advisor. Without a great handle on this area, though, you are unable to contribute to the analysis and discussion and your decisions are simply reactive.

By achieving financial security, you will understand what is happening in your business, you will be able to seize opportunities and grow wealth – both within your business and your personal life – to provide a stress-free future.

Confidently in Control

There is nothing worse than feeling like you have no control over what is happening in your business. The constant struggle of wearing too many hats, working extreme hours and being constantly at the mercy of your customers, suppliers, employees and government red tape can literally have you worn out and ready to pack it all in.

By working to control your business, rather than it controlling you, your business becomes easier to operate. You will note that I say *easier*, not *easy*. This is a critical distinction, as business is never *easy*. You can, however, create your business to be a well-managed profit machine. You call the shots. You are in charge of the key decisions on your terms. You have complete understanding of where the business is and laser focus in all areas. This is another area where the pressure that is upon you when you are overwhelmed and disorganised dissipates. No longer are you overworked and underpaid. Work flows smoothly, as does cashflow, and finally you get to the point where you can achieve that freedom that you were seeking at the start. Momentum builds and you are ready to take off to even greater heights.

Actions Taken, Ideas Implemented

When you think about where you are now in terms of having a clear plan, chances are you either have it all in your head or none exists. The ability to get distracted and off course is huge. By applying key planning concepts (covered in Chapter 6), you can head towards a stage in your business where you know exactly what needs to happen to get to your destination – and get busy achieving it.

A clear action plan allows for this. Instead of your head being filled with noise you can focus on the strategies and the actions. That's right – no more 2 am sleeplessness thinking about what you may or may not decide to target. Instead, your thoughts are all about getting it done – the actions that will see you achieve the target set. Having a plan means you won't need to worry about strategy while you should be sleeping.

It is a subtle distinction, but one that will change your business forever. It's all about setting a plan and then focusing on achieving it.

What about flexibility? Of course, things are going to change. You may exceed your target early on by being hyperactive in your actions. Conversely, you may hit a few brick walls, and need to change tack. These things also form part of your plan. It's called contingency. A business, just like a plane in flight, needs to correct its course often. However, the ultimate destination does not change. The fundamental means of getting there don't change, nor do the actions. The flight plan is just altered, or the course diverted temporarily, before getting focused back on the main game.

This ability to create a flexible yet thorough plan and follow it with focused implementation and actions provides you with the key to achieving all you set out to do in business. It is the glue that holds everything else together; a reference point, a compass, your GPS.

Case Study: Three Very Different Businesses with Three Very Different Solutions

Tony, you will recall, is a retailer who had very little idea of how his numbers worked in his business, causing both business and personal stress. By introducing Tony to the Vector Business Platform, in particular the Awareness and Numbers components, I was able to help him better understand not only his margins, but also his breakeven points. While Tony is a work in progress, his gross profit has increased by almost 10%, and he is now monitoring, and understanding, his figures monthly.

Lee, our overwhelmed signwriter, continues to work through his business management issues. Lee has cleared his backlog of overdue invoicing and quotes, and has learned how to say NO to projects that don't fit the bigger picture. He has been able to pull back his hours to a more sensible workload. Lee's biggest issue now is self-discipline and focus; however, he feels much more in control of his business, rather than it controlling him.

Stacy is our graphic designer with no plan. Stacy went through our business action plan process (described later in the book). As a result, she has a clear set of objectives, strategies and actions with implementation dates. The plan continues to change, but that's business. She just updates it and moves on.

SUMMARY

You cannot build a successful business if you focus solely on the dollars and have no idea where you want to go or what you want to achieve.

Likewise, you cannot simply focus on what you want to achieve, without actually making money.

The scientific term for a measurement that has both magnitude and direction is 'vector'. In business you need the magnitude (the money) as well as the direction (where you want to go).

The Vector Business Platform is a structured approach to achieving what you want in business. It provides the ability to move from feeling that your business and life just aren't where you want them to be, to a place where you feel as though you have achieved what you set out to do. That's when you can literally achieve an awesome business and awesome life, at whatever level that is for you.

The Vector Business Platform focuses on five key disciplines which interact to provide an annual structured approach to your business development. At the end of each year, you reset, with the first step being checking in with Awareness of where you have got to in your journey and setting renewed focus on the next destination.

It simply isn't enough to wander through small business. If you do, you will find you never achieve an awesome business and awesome life – you simply go from one distraction to the next, waking up three, five or 10 years later and wondering what the hell just happened. Structure is what is needed, and the Vector Business Platform provides that.

Now it's time to do one last important pre-flight check. Applying the Vector Business Platform requires you to understand what stage of the business cycle you are at. This is integral to each step of the platform and will ultimately guide your destination for the next 12 months.

So, let's explore. What type of business are you operating?

CHAPTER 3

YOUR BUSINESS TYPE

Before you start working on your business with the structured approach outlined in this book, you need to understand what type of business you are currently managing. I classify businesses using the following three types:

- **Go Getters:** Businesses that are either just starting out or have been recently purchased. They are at the start of the journey and will have plans centred strongly around growth and cashflow.
- **Grow Getters:** Businesses that have at least a few years of trading under their belt and have hit a wall in terms of growth or future strategy. Owners possibly know there is more out there but aren't sure how to go about achieving it.
- **Time to Go Getters:** Businesses that are ready to move on to the next stage. That may mean retirement or a change of business/industry. This type of business is heavily focused on value gap analysis, growth and systems. Becoming sale-ready is a priority.

While very different to each other, there is a common thread through all three business types: the need to design the business for ultimate exit. Business owners very rarely understand or apply this. You will recall that we touched on the purpose of a business being to generate an income as well as asset growth. With strong planning and implementation, a smart business owner will always be seeking to increase business value and maximise income.

The Vector Business Platform provides the structure for each type of business to maximise both business value and income.

As a business moves from one type to the next, the platform must be applied in a way that suits the unique features and goals related to each type.

Let's take a look at each type in detail.

GO GETTERS

If you're managing a Go Getter business, you're probably feeling a little overwhelmed at the jungle you've found yourself in as you've started to run the business. There's a whole host of things going on, and you just need some assistance to get through those early phases. The typical frustrations that I see Go Getter businesses struggling with are things like red tape; administration pressures from the ATO, ASIC, banks and lawyers; and more advice than they can handle from well-meaning friends, the guy over the fence and the woman at the pub.

If you're running a Go Getter business, everybody's trying to give you advice, the internet gurus are chiming in, and you find yourself doing Google searches to try to do it yourself – desperately trying to save a buck.

All of this becomes noise around you, and you're feeling like it's all just too much. You most likely thought this running a business thing was going to be easy. Unfortunately, there's no Business 101 course.

In the early stages of business you're trying to do things economically, so you're wearing many hats – you're likely looking after the operations, marketing, bookkeeping and staff management by yourself. You're burning the midnight oil, acting as the HR manager, the marketing manager and the finance manager. You're everything. (Phew, I'm exhausted just writing it.) Where do you get a life in all of that? Your life disappears when you're at the Go Getter stage. You jump in with both feet, all guns blazing and you're doing everything that you can to make this whole thing work.

Much of your time is spent cautiously managing the business financials as you're not at a stage where you're making an adequate level of profitability. You're making sure that you're not putting money towards perceived non-essentials. Sometimes that's a short-sighted view, though, because there are some investments that could take you to that next stage more quickly.

The fact is, you don't really understand what it is that you're looking at when you're managing your financials. You're just measuring the amount of money that's in the bank. Go Getters rarely have a budget, which results in poor cashflow management.

If you're one of the Go Getters who has bought a business, maybe you're a little bit more advanced – but you're probably still feeling that overwhelm. Despite buying a pre-existing business, you don't know where it's going to go now. It becomes essential to watch it closely in the first 12 months of operation, to make sure that it does what the label said it would when you bought it. Typically, you've got debt involved in buying the business, and feel frustrated that you need to be so focused on things financially, when all you want is to be able to get in and run the business.

Go Getters don't go into business or buy a business to be tied up with all of the administration. Go Getters want to get in and be Go Getters. They want to go places, fast.

Personally, I love working with business owners in this phase because of that ambition. Go Getters have a desire to get stuck into the action; they want to put in the work, rather than having a magic wand waved over the business. Go Getters want to build their business. They want to develop a team and get the structure and culture of their business in place.

If you're a Go Getter, it might be a hard pill to swallow when you realise you have to crawl before you can walk. It's important to harness your ambition, and focus it in the right direction, otherwise it just scatters around thinly in all different places.

The Go Getter also wants to enjoy the benefits of the business – but they know they must survive the first 12 to 24 months first. During that period, in an attempt to conserve funds, they don't draw a wage. This can be a mistake. While it may not be possible right away, the sooner you can actually be drawing a commercial wage for the effort you're putting in the better. Remember, a business is an income generator as well as an asset that you will grow in value. It's an investment.

Having a clear focus from the start is critical. What is it that you're trying to achieve within the first 12 to 18 months? Let's set some targets around that and work out how you are going to achieve them.

Then, when you get there, you can sit back and say, 'We did what we set out to do.' This is at the core of the Vector Business Platform.

How do you go about this? Here are some of the things that you need to be looking at:

- **Structure:** By getting great advice at the start, you can ensure you are getting the right business structure for you. Many business owners go in with the simplest and least expensive structure, which actually can be the best option initially – overcomplicating things can make it more expensive and also more complex than needed. Your business may not be at the stage where you're going to need a complex structure like a company or a trust for a few years, so you can hold back on that. However, depending on the industry you are in or the assets you hold, risk may be a priority for you. Unfortunately, consideration of the right structure is often an afterthought or based on what a 'mate' told you to do. My thoughts? Get great advice from a professional at this crucial stage.

- **Planning:** It's crucial that you create not just a business plan, but a plan that's going to give you definite actions. It needs to be a living and breathing map for your business for the first few years. It's very easy to keep your plans in your head. But when you keep your plans in your head, they're very easily changed, and you're not held accountable to what's in there. When you're always changing your plans, chaos starts to happen, causing you to feel uncomfortable because things are uncertain. I recommend investing in getting great advice at the planning stage. Yes, you can get a template online, but then you need to actually complete it. Great advice at this stage pays for itself in terms of achieving early results, rather than getting 12 to 18 months down the track and wondering what happened.

- **Support and advice:** A great accountant, coach or advisor is of massive value to Go Getters, as their nature means that they're ambitious, and have so many great ideas running through their heads. There's so much passion and so many thoughts that they often need tempering with another viewpoint. A great advisor will help a Go Getter through those periods where they need a sounding board; when they ask themselves, 'Is this a great idea or am I completely off my rocker?'

Case Study: Purchasing a Business

Tom was referred to me for help reviewing figures on a business he was purchasing. Being new to business, Tom, who is quite savvy and curious, knew that getting good advice early was critical. As part of my analysis and subsequent due diligence, I was able to provide him with the information to negotiate approximately $300,000 off the original business asking price. I also helped Tom secure finance with a business plan and cashflow forecast as well as with his choice of business structure and implementation of accounting software. Tom is a Go Getter, with plenty of ideas and motivation to grow his business, and I am sure he will climb through the ranks as he achieves his targets.

GROW GETTERS

At some point, every small business owner reaches a fork in the road. Maybe you hit a wall in terms of growth or decide it's time to change tack and come up with a new line of work or strategy.

Whether it's growing pains such as increased costs, staff issues or cashflow needs or the need to achieve the next level of sales growth in key markets, you get to the stage where you know you want more, but you need some guidance on how to get there. Change management and accountability become critical to your success.

Let's have a closer look at what typically frustrates a Grow Getter.

When a business is new and fresh, the desire to chase and attract work is high. There is a hunger, typically driven by financial need, to grow quickly – an eagerness that is very hard to maintain as the business grows. If you're the new kid on the block, your ability to attract new business is often high. However, when those first few heady years are over, the hard work begins. Often, pricing becomes an issue as you are no longer new or buying your way into work. It's time to make solid money, but how do you structure a price increase without losing old customers?

A business that has been in existence for a while can hit multiple walls. Each wall you hit takes a different approach and a new set of thinking to get over than the last.

As a Grow Getter, you might find it hard to maintain quality standards as you take on additional team members and create systems on the fly. You're trying to scale beyond yourself, but it feels like the plane is being built while it's in the air. This affects your stress and workloads. The ability to scale is crucial for growth but the move from owner to manager and leader can often be difficult for those with no training or experience.

The business is normally now at a stage where it has a mix of customers or clients. There are the original clients – typically lower value and at times lower quality – as well as the new, bright and shiny clients that are probably spending more and providing much more fulfilling work.

Cashflow rears its head again as additional team members means additional wages. You're not only responsible for your own livelihood, but also the livelihoods of your team members. This is the time I often see owners revert to paying themselves less until things level out again. The cycle then continues, as to get more cashflow, the business needs to achieve more growth. To achieve more growth requires more focus on additional customers. That's more time for the owner to wear yet another hat.

What a whirlwind business has become.

As a Grow Getter, you are now wanting to be able to delegate more work, and have that work done to a high standard. You are most likely now seeking additional funding from the bank to help with your business growth. To achieve everything you are trying to achieve, it is critical that you have a clear plan in place. Without a clear plan, the many plates you have spinning are likely to fall.

To ensure that all of this can be done, here are some things that Grow Getters should focus on:

- **Quality financials:** Generating and understanding a quality set of management and statutory financials is essential. These should not just be for the purpose of getting your tax done. No business has ever had a tax problem without profit. The quality financial information will allow you to make key decisions based on solid data, as well as become lending-ready when funds are required.
- **Procedures and systems:** It is critical to build strong procedures and systems to make sure your business can scale. Putting a team in place without strong procedures reduces team members' satisfaction and your ability to delegate tasks. Poor-quality work is normally the result of poor systems rather than poor employees. If the problem *is*

poor employees, you need a system to performance-manage them – with the aim of getting things on track, or, if that's not possible, taking corrective action early.

- **A clear plan and accountability structure:** Focus is essential for a Grow Getter. To focus you need to follow a strong action plan. With definitive actions, both yourself and your team members will be able to master implementation. When you take action, results happen. A plan, however, is only half the picture. It's easy to be distracted away from implementation when you're busy with the day-to-day running of the show. A strong accountability structure will provide focus on the key drivers of the business, allow you to review the action plan, and also provide the opportunity for a sounding board, motivation and of course a bit of carrot-and-stick discipline.

If you are a Grow Getter, the Vector Business Platform's key disciplines of Numbers, Planning, Improvement and Accountability will have a huge influence.

You are likely to need to focus on resetting your goals – the things you want to achieve – now that you are running a more mature business. When you're working on processes and systems, a good starting point is to brain dump your workflows and create or improve each one as you go. Prioritising and chunking down your plans and actions will prove essential as you simply cannot achieve everything in one sitting.

Case Study: Growing Pains

Karl and Christine run a successful building company.

As their long-term coach and accountant, I have seen them grow from humble beginnings to exceeding sales targets in the last couple of years – a ceiling they had struggled to break through previously. Their success took them into another tier in business: they became Grow Getters. This meant they required larger premises, more complex business and tax structures and more touchpoints for great advice. Their cashflow circles became bigger as demand for their product grew and their team expanded in sync. These growing pains required strong planning, cashflow management and sounding board advice and accountability to ensure things got done and focus stayed strong – all of which my team and I were able to provide.

TIME TO GO GETTERS

There is nothing more certain in this world – well, okay, death and taxes – but third on the list has to be the fact that at some point, you will want to exit your business. When you become a Time to Go Getter, it can be for a wide range of reasons.

Perhaps you have another challenge or opportunity to pursue, or perhaps it's time to retire. Maybe you are being forced to get out either financially or because of poor health or personal tragedy or loss.

Whatever the reason, Time to Go Getters exhibit some key traits.

The first of these is the fact that your single biggest asset, outside of your home, is likely to be your business. Following years of hard work, your next biggest pool of wealth is superannuation – but if you're not ready to retire, this is largely inaccessible. There is normally a level of debt also associated with a business at this stage, and your business is probably your sole source of income.

What that means is that when you choose to either move on to the next challenge or retire, it is critical that you get the maximum value for your business. There are two concepts that matter when it comes to exit strategies: your magic number, and your business value.

Your Magic Number

Your magic number is the amount of capital you need to take your next step. You may be considering starting or purchasing a different business; or perhaps you are retiring, and your business represents your nest egg.

Have you actually given thought as to what you would like to achieve when exiting your business, and how much money you will need? What future events will need funding? Children's education, weddings, investment, holidays, an extended period of not working? All of these need to be taken into account.

Existing debt is often another major consideration, with many naïve small business owners attempting to sell their business to cover what they owe plus a buffer. I regularly see scenarios like this and they never work.

Having said that, if your magic number equals debt plus buffer, then that, rightly or wrongly, is your magic number. Where it becomes interesting is when we compare that magic number to your business value.

Your Business Value

It is essential to know what your business is worth, and how to calculate this. In basic terms, a business is valued based on its profitability and its apparent risk level. The more profitable a business, the higher its value. The less risky a business, the higher its value. The converse is also the case. Obviously, there are outliers, like startups or tech companies, that defy this logic, however the majority of businesses follow this rationale.

By understanding your business value, you can be better pre-pared for when the time to go arrives. The aim is to have your business value align with your magic number. If your magic number is higher than your business value, you have what is called a value gap (see figure 3.1). In other words, what you seek to be paid for your business, upon exit, far outweighs the reality. When you have a value gap you have two options: either reduce the funds available for your next step – that is, your magic number – or increase your business value.

Figure 3.1: Value Gap

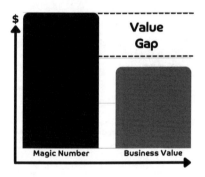

If your business value exceeds your magic number, congratula-tions! You have a value surplus (see figure 3.2). However, maybe it's time to go back and reconsider what it is that you want to exit your business for, dollar-wise. This can be in the form of expanding your bucket list or expanding your philanthropic or purpose-driven activities.

It is the continual assessment of both the magic number and your business value that is key here. As you embark on your busi-ness improvement journey by applying the concepts in this book, you will find the needle will move on both. Your first job is to assess each component, then quantify any gap that exists.

If a gap exists, you will need to consider various options of bridging the gap to ensure that when it is time to go, you are in the best financial position possible.

Figure 3.2: Value Surplus

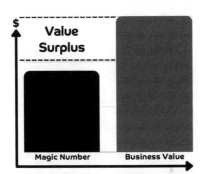

Case Study: When it's Time to Go

Bruce and Carlene were my long-term clients and operated a very successful home nursing business. They engaged my assistance when they were approached by a company that wished to acquire them. They were firmly in Time to Go Getter mode. The negotiation process extended almost 12 months before falling over. We quickly moved to holding a strategic planning session to map out what was required to make the business more attractive to a future buyer, which set in motion a two-year process – including our chairing of a board of advice. The board of advice allowed us to provide monthly board meetings, often involving other relevant advisors, giving a more corporate approach to decision-making than what is often found in a typical Mum and Dad scenario. The board of advice provided significant implementation focus, culminating in a successful sale and ultimate retirement for Bruce and Carlene. Without the focus on the strategic side of the business, the sale, and retirement, would have taken much longer to achieve.

SUMMARY

Each of the three business types, while unique in their own right, have some common themes. No matter where you fit, it's a matter of:

- Understanding where you are now, and where you want to be
- Determining actions required to get there
- Embarking on constant improvement
- Developing a strong accountability structure
- Committing to annual reassessment.

These common threads are all part of the Vector Business Platform. While these common threads exist, each business type will approach them slightly differently.

For example, a Go Getter will be focused on developing structure, high growth and early wins as opposed to a Grow Getter, who is focused on team development and further growth in defined areas of their business. A Time to Go Getter may be focused on systems and sustainable profitability, becoming sale-ready in the process. All of these require different strategies and actions.

When it comes to accountability, a Go Getter may be requiring accountability for themselves only. More mature businesses – Grow Getters and Time to Go Getters – will have teams that also need an accountability structure, as well as amplified, more complex issues to deal with regularly.

Understanding what type you are, then, needs to be considered before you embark on the content in Part II. Take time now to consider whether you are a Go Getter, a Grow Getter or a Time to Go Getter. Wear your current badge with pride, and when you are ready, it's time to take flight with Part II.

PART II
TAKING FLIGHT

The seatbelt sign has now been turned on. It's time to get the next 12 months of your business journey started. This section will take you through the detail of the Vector Business Platform. This structured approach will ensure you arrive at your destination in great shape. Make no mistake: this journey will not be easy. Expect a bit of turbulence, as well as feeling restless in your seat at times. Stay the course, follow the process and you'll make it to Part III: Arrivals. Let's take flight.

CHAPTER 4

AWARENESS

Awareness is defined as, 'Being knowledgeable or well informed about a particular situation.' When I talk about awareness with respect to your business, I am simply saying that you must understand where you are now, where you want to go and how you are going to get there. If you're fully aware of your situation and your surroundings, you can create a plan of action to deal with anything.

Awareness needs to come before anything else in your business. Without a solid understanding of your current situation and needs, you will exhaust a great deal of energy working on things that are just not relevant. As you move past your needs, understanding where you sit financially with both your business value and key numbers becomes vital. This is irrespective of which business type you resonated with in Chapter 3.

If you compare where you are wanting to go with where you are now, there will undoubtedly be gaps. These gaps are what you will work on over the coming months. Bridging these gaps is evidence of progress towards your goals. You will achieve more, and gain immense satisfaction, as you start to move towards your end destination.

Awareness also provides you with the opportunity to explore a number of scenarios, and perform 'what-if' modelling for your business. Finding hidden profit opportunities is a great motivator, as having some early wins fuels confidence and will fire you up to achieve more.

UNDERSTANDING YOUR NEEDS

When commencing the structured development of your business, you can burn a great deal of time by focusing on the wrong things. Given many business owners list lack of time as a concern, I am constantly amazed at how many coaching programs are not designed with the needs of the business owner front and centre. I call this taking a textbook approach. The problem with a textbook approach is that there is no focus on what really matters to *you*. If what you need is not contained between pages one and 150 of the coaching manual, well, tough luck. It's often passed off as a systemised approach. Unfortunately, most of these approaches are cookie cutter and simply don't respect your time, or your investment.

So how do you approach determining your needs? Who asks the questions? How do you ensure you uncover the full picture?

The first resource I would like to introduce you to is the Vector Business Scorecard. At the heart of the Vector Business Scorecard is the concept of four key stages of small business. Each stage has been built around the analogy of flying, similar to the core parts of this book. As you move through each stage, you face new challenges which, if conquered, progress you to the next stage. Your aim? Progress. Your ultimate goal is formed by your needs,

and directly linked to the things you set out to do when you originally started out in business.

Let's take a look at the four stages.

1. Stalled

You can't move forward in your business without momentum. At
this stage, you feel like you are stuck, not making any progress
and a bit lost as to what to do next. This can be corrected with
some simple solutions based around the five areas of the Vector
Business Platform. Every business is different, and how solutions
are developed also varies greatly.

2. In Motion

You have either been in business a while and you're finding it
hard to get to the next stage, or you are new to business and
moving through the ranks.

You are moving, building momentum, yet need to ensure
everything is done consistently and correct the first time around
rather than creating a monster that will become too hard to tame.

As you progress through the In Motion stage you will be focusing on higher sales, higher profits and higher surplus cashflow;
however, you will also be dealing with higher complexity.

3. In Flight

You have either been at it a while and you're now looking towards
more challenges, or you are reasonably new and moved through
the ranks fast, and now have growing pains. You have probably
achieved some great successes, yet feel that there is more to do.
Problem is, you're not quite sure how to get there. This stage is
much harder than the stages you have now left behind you.

The good thing is that the air is clearer up here, and all these things are signs of a successful business. It's time to reach for At Altitude status, and there is a definite path to take with the Vector Business Platform. Every business is different, and how your solutions are developed and how you travel your path also varies greatly. The platform has been designed to ensure you can access a tailored approach to your business advice while being supported with a solid structure.

4. At Altitude

You are in some rare air here! It takes some real grit and determination to not only get here, but also stay.

It's likely that you have either been here a while and you're contemplating what's next, you're finding it hard to stay at this level with issues such as staff and complexity creeping in, or you are new to the alumni, having moved through the ranks fast and now having some growing pains and/or big plans.

Either way, your aim in the short term should be to ensure each of the five disciplines of the Vector Business Platform are At Altitude, if they're not already. From there, the aim is to maintain the rage, and work each area. It's all about consistent improvement and maintenance.

The biggest-ticket priorities I see at this level are asset protection, structure and tax, estate planning and succession/transition planning.

These four business stages are yet another example of why every business is different. Every business has unique needs. Without taking the time to understand what type of business you are managing – Go Getter, Grow Getter or Time to Go Getter – and then determining where you are at in the cycle of each – Stalled,

In Motion, In Flight or At Altitude – your specific needs just get lost in the fog.

This can lead to you spending years focused on all the wrong things, as you are guided by well-meaning parties fitting you into their process, rather than the other way around.

Take time now to go to **direction.com.au/vectorbusinessscore** and complete your first Vector Business Scorecard. This will provide you with your business score and let you know which of the above stages your business is at. At the end of your first run-through of *Awesome Business Awesome Life* (including your implementation), I encourage you to again complete the scorecard and compare THEN to where you are NOW.

WHAT'S YOUR BUSINESS WORTH?

I'd like to restate the reason you are in business: you are in business to make a profit (income stream) as well as grow an asset (your business value). All other reasons for having a business come as a result of making money and growing value. Money and value are the enablers of your future objectives. A business cannot be a force for good if it does not have surplus funds.

Increasing business value requires real thinking about future needs. The first and most obvious reason for building business value is that of retirement. For most business owners, their business is their most valuable asset outside their home. Yet not enough attention is given to increasing its value, with its ultimate sale more of an afterthought once the decision to retire is made. This is resulting in a massive wealth loss among small business owners, and the economy as a whole.

Perhaps you are not ready to retire and are instead looking towards your next venture, whatever that may be. How much money will that next venture require? How many years will you be in that new venture? What will the next step need to look like when you do decide retirement is the next option?

Or possibly you could be forced out of business through ill health or family circumstances. Ensuring that you are consistently focused on building business value from the start will mean you are not caught short if unexpected events arise.

Awareness of where your business is at value-wise is typically avoided when it comes to these tough decisions. In fact, we avoid NOT being in business a bit like death: we know it is going to happen yet believe it will never happen to us... Yeah, right.

Everything, and I mean everything, in your business needs to be transparent and known.

What is the end game? Let's become aware of these things and let's get serious with our goals. What would your business be worth if you had to sell today? Do you know the answer?

I have been involved in many business sales and the fact is that most owners decide their business price from the inside out. They look at the debt that needs to be cleared, the holiday that comes after the sale and the funds needed to tuck away for retirement.

Problem is, this results in a significantly overvalued business. This leads to a lengthy time on the market, and also results in a flawed analysis of what the true needs will be post-business.

How to Value Your Business

For now, we are going to take a non-technical view of business valuation. There are a number of great books on the technical aspects of valuation – many that will have your brain melting at the complexity involved (we often provide complex profes-sional business valuations for clients in areas such as family law or investment matters). However, that is not what you need at this point in your journey. What you need is a simple, practical way of assessing your business's value – one that you can use as an annual benchmark for your business, as well as the basis for decisions around where to improve. Once you've arrived at a firm idea of value, you can address the key areas that may be bringing the value down and make necessary improvements.

As I mentioned in Chapter 3, business value, at its heart, is a combination of profitability and risk. The most common methods used to value businesses are the Future Maintainable Earnings (FME) method and Net Tangible Assets (NTA) method. Industries also typically have rules of thumb that are used as guides, normally based on a multiple of revenue. When we conduct a Business Value Discovery as part of the Awareness discipline in the Vector Business Platform, we primarily use the FME method, using NTA and rules of thumb as comparisons only.

In a private market, business value can sometimes feel irrelevant, as a sale takes two parties, buyer and seller, and each party's advisors are typically working from a position of proving a valuation incorrect as opposed to correct. The purpose of understanding your business's value, from the perspective of working your way through the Vector Business Platform, is to improve your business on the key drivers, benchmarking your business either against your own annual progress or others in the market. Any ultimate sale calculation will be far more technical. It is why I often refer to this valuation as being a 'back of a beer coaster' valuation.

The FME method uses a weighted average of a figure called Earnings before Interest, Tax, Depreciation and Amortisation (EBITDA). When it comes to privately owned small businesses, I strongly advocate that any EBITDA figure should include a commercial wage for the owner's labour efforts. To not provide for this in the earnings figure would see it over inflated, not giving a true measure of the return on your investment in the business. Owners' wages are a reward for effort. Profit, or EBITDA, is a reward for invested funds. This distinction is vital.

Once we have the weighted average EBITDA, we then apply a multiple to this figure. The multiple is based on risk factors. I will cover risk in detail in Chapter 6; however, the basic premise is that the riskier the business is, the lower the multiple. As an example, a multiple of two would be indicating that the business purchase price could be recouped from profits in two years. Similarly, a multiple of four would be indicating it would take four years to recoup the price. Now, if a business is riskier, you want to recoup your money quicker, correct? Of course you do. Conversely, if the business is steady and strong, you will be prepared to wait a little longer. While this is a simplistic view of risk and multiples, it forms the basis for understanding how perceived risk affects your business value.

Now, if we think about the two factors that affect value – profit (or EBITDA) and risk – we can see how value can be improved. Lower risk, higher value. Higher profitability, higher value. This, then, is where working on improving your business becomes critical: improve profitability and work on mitigating risk. This recipe for increasing the value of your second most valuable asset can have a massive impact on your business and personal life.

Other Factors Impacting Value

The value of a business can divert from the traditional valuation drivers depending on the type of buyer. Take for instance e-commerce or tech-based businesses. Quite often, these businesses rank very poorly on traditional measures such as profitability and risk. If the buyer, however, perceives value in the company's market share, irrespective of profitability, this can bring a premium. A buyer may also be a large corporate, purely interested in a volume play irrespective of costs and systems. Identifying WHO your future buyer is can help you build a strategy around maximising and highlighting what that buyer is seeking.

Another factor that can create buying desire is the ability to take time off from the business. If your business model dictates that you, as the owner, need to be tied to the business and working unrealistic hours week in, week out, you are going to find it very hard to make your business attractive to a future buyer. Less attractive, lower value. Being ready for the question 'How many hours do you work in the business?' can really assist when negotiations get to the pointy end.

This is not a quick fix, as you will see, and real improvement of business value should be carried out over the mid term by following the steps outlined in the Vector Business Platform.

Remember that the key is to be aware and be prepared.

Case Study: Getting Sale-Ready

James and Georgie, a husband-and-wife team, owned a retail business. They ran a great business, assisted by two employees. Despite my initial urging over many years to cement their systems and processes with a view to eventually sell, James measured much of the business performance in a trusty notebook, while Georgie manoeuvred her way through the suppliers' endless order processes and materials. The business worked, for them. However, when the time came to sell, it became evident that it needed to work for others. The first attempt to sell saw the prospective buyer get cold feet when it got to contract stage, as he could not see himself running the business day-to-day. Through a process of constant improvement, James and Georgie were able to address issues such as systems and procedures, pricing, ordering, stock levels and profitability, which ensured that when the next buyer arrived, the business was sale-ready and appropriately valued. James and Georgie are now enjoying retired life, having secured a successful sale. The new owners, to my knowledge, continue to operate a successful business.

BRIDGING THE VALUE GAP

As an accountant and business coach, I often speak to business owners who are unsure about what will happen when the day comes to get out.

Yes, it's going to happen. Whether it's by choice or forced upon you, the day will come when you just won't want to – or possibly won't be able to – be in your business anymore.

So what are your choices? Sell? Transfer ownership to a colleague or family member? Pull down the shutters and walk away?

Too often I come across business owners who have failed to plan and end up having a business valued at significantly less than what is needed for their next step.

As covered briefly in Chapter 3, I call this the value gap.

The value gap is the difference between your magic number – the amount of money you wish to have available for your next step, whether that be business, or personal – and your business value.

The earlier you focus on being aware of, and bridging, the value gap, the better. Planning starts many years before the day you exit the business.

The Australian Bureau of Statistics estimates that over 40% of business owners will be looking to exit their business over the next five years. This is considered to be due to baby boomers retiring and represents a massive shifting of wealth in the Australian economy (see table 4.1).

Table 4.1: Key Small Business Statistics

Number of Australian businesses 2018	2.4 million
Percentage employing four or fewer people	89%
Percentage with turnover < $2 million	93%
Percentage looking to exit within five years	40%

Source: Australian Bureau of Statistics counts of Australian business, August 2021.

Some business owners will not be so lucky, though. They will reach the stage of exiting before they are sale-ready, and many won't even understand the concept of getting their business to that stage. Understanding your value gap early allows you to take action in an orderly fashion and increase the value of your business, and in turn your wealth.

So how do you bridge the value gap?

Firstly, you can tweak your magic number. Considerations might include:

- **Downsizing your home:** Will you require less space in future and therefore sell the family home, resulting in a capital inflow or debt reduction?
- **Future income needs:** Working with a financial planner early can make a huge difference here.

- **Current investments and increases pre-retirement:**
  More investment outside of your business will improve
  your retirement lifestyle.
- **Whether your 'next step' is well planned and
  appropriately priced.**

The difficulty with your magic number is that you can usually
only tweak it so far before diminishing what you want to achieve.
None of us want to compromise our future. It's therefore normally
much more beneficial to focus on increasing business value.

As I outlined earlier in this chapter, business value is a function of profitability and risk. The higher the profitability and the
lower the risk, the greater the business value.

Much of the work that needs to be performed to improve the
value of your business needs to be part of a clear plan. A great
plan will ask three key questions:

1. Where are you now?
2. Where do you need to be?
3. How are you going to get there?

A good way to do this is to engage in a facilitated planning
session, where you can flesh out your objectives and set the strategies to achieve them. These sessions are a great opportunity to
throw mud at the wall and see what sticks. Following a strategic
planning session you are in a perfect position to develop your
business action plan (more on this in Chapter 6), which will help
you achieve all the areas identified as necessary.

The next step in the planning process is to set budgets and
forecasts. Many business owners I come into contact with don't
like the restriction of a set budget – they like to think more on

their feet. For business improvement work, the key is to not only have traditional profit-and-loss-style budgets but also have forecasts around the key drivers in your business. You must be able to answer the following questions:

- What is your forecast level of sales for each division in your business?
- What is your targeted average sale?
- What actions need to happen to drive that? (Leading indicators.)

There are many key drivers that need forecasting and this planning is crucial. 'What-if' scenarios can be run in line with business value analysis to set realistic targets for improvement; once set, the key is to have accountability to those targets. Accountability will not only keep you on track but also provide real-world motivation to make things happen. It can also provide you with ways of attacking the common challenges that occur when making change in a business. I'll go through the most common accountability styles I work on with clients in Chapter 8.

Systems and Effectiveness

Improving your business systems and effectiveness has a huge impact on perceived risk factors and therefore business value. A business that can be replicated by someone new to your industry will be worth multiples of one that isn't easily replicated. For a purchaser, the ability to gain efficiencies from day one is critical. Mature businesses tend to have high reliance on owners and have often reached a comfort level that breeds inefficient processes and labour. Corrections to these areas can bring great results.

Structure

The old 'working ON your business' mantra allows an owner to pull back from their business. You should aim to adopt some variant of a corporate culture in your business. Moving back from the coalface allows a structure that is succession-friendly and, as a result, value increases.

Key to this though is moving back at the right time. Delegating fully, too soon, can delay realisation of strong profits by many years.

Mindset

What happens when an owner does not fully believe what can be achieved? Or when they know what can be achieved, but are too tired to continue?

At the other extreme, what happens when an owner simply cannot visualise their business ever achieving, and they just want out?

The human mind is a complex creature. It's often necessary for business owners to need to overcome mindset barriers, enabling them to move on to bigger and better things. This is a specialised area that your coach, if you have one, will work closely on with you. I like to work with clients in this area as part of the Accountability section of the Vector Business Platform. We will cover more on this important area in Chapter 8.

HIDDEN PROFITS AND EASY WINS

It's human nature to want things straight away. We have become a very impatient society. In a world of instant gratification, if something is not working straight away we tend to lose interest quickly. Business is no different.

As you start your journey along the Vector Business Platform, you will most likely seek this instant gratification. It's important, then, that you have a quick-wins process to get you moving. Being able to find some hidden profits, while working through your awareness of the key numbers, gives you a huge burst of enthusiasm to launch you into the next stages. Everyone loves achieving results, so let's explore how to do it.

American marketing whiz Jay Abraham first introduced the concept of the three ways to grow any business. Since it became popular, any advisor worth their salt has used a variation of that work as a means to show a business owner how to grow. As part of the Vector Business Platform, we have designed our own hidden profits analysis using five key drivers, allowing you to build what-if scenarios around the key areas of your business. You will soon see that to achieve great early wins, the changes you need to make are minimal.

Hidden profits is all about what-if modelling. What-if modelling takes your current trading figures and creates additional improvement scenarios. One of the best ways to use what-if modelling is to break trading results down into key components.

For example, revenue can be broken down into:

Number of Customers × Average Sale

Modelling can be performed to look at what would happen if:

- Customer numbers increased by 2%
- Conversion rate improved by 2%
- Average sale to each customer improved by 5%.

Beyond quick wins, profitability has a huge bearing on business value, and therefore, modelling potential profitability improvement allows a business owner to actually visualise it happening, rather than improvement simply being a pie in the sky. Analysis of profit margins and pricing can also glean some massive gains for business. Such is the power of knowing your numbers.

While most businesses now understand that pricing can be increased with very little negative effect, too few are actually implementing this strategy. Even more confusing are the businesses that continually discount to 'bring in the volume'. That's fine if you are running a department store or supermarket, but it's insanity for the average small business. The numbers prove this. If you are unsure, you can check out the proof at: **direction.com. au/pricing-charts**.

Some significant improvements can be gained by analysing margins on products and also the mix of sales in your business. Selling more of your most profitable products is key. Too often, though, it is a large volume of low-margin work that keeps small business owners overworked and underpaid.

Let's take a look at how to apply the hidden profits analysis.

Profitability is simply a mathematical calculation. If you can use the multiplication button on a calculator, you can work out how to increase your profits. Obviously it's the hard work and strategies behind those improvements that make the magic happen, but hang in here… this stuff works. The calculation looks a little like this:

Number of Leads
(the number of potential buyers who contact you)
× Conversion Rate
(the percentage of leads who purchase from you)
= Number of Customers
× Number of Times they Buy
(how many times they buy from you, on average,
in the period being measured – normally a year)

× Average Sale Value
(average amount each customer spends on each sale)
= Total Sales
× Profit Margin
(this can be measured on either a gross or net profit basis
and represents how efficient you are in delivering your
service/product)
= PROFIT

Now the key is to insert your CURRENT figures into each component of the calculation. Don't worry if you don't have these figures as yet. This is half the exercise. Figures don't calculate correctly? Again, this is part of your learning. If you don't know these numbers, you need to. Your accounting system should have all the information you need. If it doesn't, don't worry – it soon will, as we will be covering that in the next chapter.

Once you have your current figures in, it is time to do some exploring. What would happen if:

- You increased your leads by 2%? OR
- You increased your conversion rate by 2%?

Put the book down for a second and try changing things around in different combinations and see the end result at the bottom of the page. Once you have a scenario you are happy with, stop there, come back and read on… don't worry, I'll still be here.

How did you go? Did you get a figure you are happy with for now?

Now, I want you to look at each component and ask yourself, *how could I achieve that?* If it is an increase in leads, how could you make that happen? More advertising? Better pitching of what you do? More attractive product or offering?

There is a wealth of strategies that can be used to increase each component, so take some time now to plot out your thinking on each. Here are some examples:

- **Number of leads:** Traditional advertising, social media, search engine optimisation (SEO), networking, formal referral programs.
- **Conversion rate:** Improved sales process, improved customer follow-up and nurturing, content creation, focused product offerings, improved customer experience, improved quotes.
- **Number of times they buy:** Loyalty programs, easily accessible entry price points, product/service mix.
- **Average sale value:** Upselling/cross selling, increased prices, service knowledge, product/service mix, selling to the correct target market.
- **Profit margin:** Cost analysis, supplier alternatives, bulk buying, reduced wastage, procedures and systems, smaller premises, offshore staff.

Take some time to note, next to each component, some ideas on how you are going to achieve these changes. These initial quick wins are designed to fuel your thinking for your bigger-picture plan that we will cover in Chapter 6.

SUMMARY

Awareness is all about being knowledgeable or well informed about your business – understanding where you are now, where you want to go and how you are going to get there.

To achieve awareness, you must look at your business needs: the areas that your business has to prioritise over all others to achieve your goals. Quite often, a business owner does not know what they don't know, so a thorough analysis of your needs has to be performed.

I introduced to you the concept of the Vector Business Scorecard, the first step in understanding where your business currently sits in its journey. For the scorecard, we use the analogy of a flight, with a business being either Stalled, In Motion, In Flight or At Altitude.

Deeper needs analysis with your key advisor is hugely beneficial once you have completed the scorecard, to delve further into specific areas of focus.

Assessing your current business value and the concept of your magic number gives you some defined yardsticks to measure your business by. The combination of these two measurements allows you to determine your value gap: a key figure no matter the stage your business is in. The more time you have to bridge the gap, the better.

Once you are aware of your value gap, you can perform what-if scenarios to add to your thought processes, and begin formulating your plan of attack. This is not your full plan, but a plan to achieve some quick wins. This builds confidence and motivation to forge through a full 12-month business development cycle. It also provides a basic introduction to how integral numbers are to creating an awesome business and awesome life.

CHAPTER 5

NUMBERS

I am always highly amused when, upon hearing I am an accountant, people say, 'Oh you must have been good at maths.' Now, I don't doubt that accountants are numbers people, but other than basic maths, there is not a lot of other application. As a small business advisor, it's not like I am breaking out some calculus or Pythagoras's theorem at every opportunity.

Business numbers, though, and a great understanding as to how they help you make key decisions in business, are a prerequisite for a great business advisor, as well as a business owner. In fact, I'd go as far as to say that having a great understanding of business numbers should be a prerequisite for going into business in the first place.

Before we get into the meat of this chapter, I'd like to point out that if you are an experienced business owner – maybe a Grow Getter or Time to Go Getter – you may find some (not all) of this content a bit basic. If this is you, I want you to approach the chapter as a refresher. I guarantee that you will take away at least two new insights as to how to apply numbers in your business. And if you don't, well, I'll shout you a one-on-one, FREE advanced numbers session, to make sure you do.

Numbers are the backbone of a business. They provide a record of what has happened and an insight into what will. You can use numbers to provide what-if scenarios, and in turn set strategies around those. Business numbers can be used to track progress and analyse problems. They are also used to verify transactions and ensure accuracy and completeness. They are at the heart of your business value and consequently your wealth.

This chapter will take you through understanding your numbers in a practical way, with the outcome of being able to interpret your financials and have higher levels of conversation with your advisors. As part of understanding your numbers, I will guide you through the essentials of getting on top of your tax. We will also look at creating your business money plan: your flexible forecast of profit and cashflow for the next 12 months, and beyond. Lastly, we will ensure that you are able to keep great-quality bookwork in a fraction of the time you are spending now, through automating your essential tasks and workflows.

Numbers are at the heart of your business; understanding them will make a seismic shift in how you operate.

BUSINESS FINANCIALS 101

Think about all the different hats you wear in your business – the production hat, the sales hat, the marketing hat, the customer service hat, the technology hat and the financial controller hat. Which hat is usually the most uncomfortable? For most of my clients, it's the financial controller hat. Why? Because it's the hat that you're least likely to have had any training in.

Understanding business financial management isn't something that comes naturally. It is something that is learned, and unless someone has shown you how to do it before, you can't be expected to know all about it. It is a very important hat, however. An understanding of your business's financial performance and your financial position is crucial to being able to make appropriate decisions about how you do business. It will make or break your success.

While success means different things to different people, business success is chiefly financial. A business's success is measured by its profitability, the return on assets, the return on the owner's investment. The money created is an enabler for your life.

Take a few moments to ask yourself:

- How do I currently measure my business's performance?
- Do I leave the financial management of my business to someone else? (Note: this is the *financial management*, NOT the bookkeeping.) Who does that part?
- Do I already know how profitable my business is before I receive my year-end financial statements from my accountant?

With the pace of change in regulations, the economic environment and technology – and statistics that show 39% of small business owners see the sale of their business as their primary source of retirement funds – you cannot afford to leave your business's financial management unchecked. It's *your* business and its success rests with the financial decisions you make.

Mark Twain said, 'Courage is resistance to fear, mastery of fear, not absence of fear' – so don't worry if you're a little daunted by the financial side of your business.

UNDERSTANDING YOUR PROFIT AND LOSS

Profit is most basically defined as income less expenses. It is the measure of performance over a period of time in a business: that is, profit and loss for the year ended 30 June 20XX.

It is probably even more important to realise what profit is *not*. Profit is not money in less money out. This distinction is important, as profit does not directly correlate to the movements in your bank account – some of which may be working capital flows.

Profit is used as a basis for taxation. When most businesses talk of profit, they relate it to how much tax they will be liable for. While tax is an important factor, it should not be the primary focus for a successful business.

As a business owner, you need to know how your business is performing over a period of time so you can take actions to improve and achieve your targets.

By analysing a profit and loss statement, a great deal of information can be gained about how your business is running. It may highlight overruns in expenses, high wage levels in relation to turnover, decreasing profit margins or downturn in revenue. The interaction between its components is also important.

If you just measured your performance by sales levels, you may think you're doing great during a period of sales growth, but that growth may not be translating to higher profits. You need to be able to read your profit and loss statement to identify why.

You use profit to measure the performance of your business against others, against budget, and to show your business's capacity to make money. Your business's capacity to make money impacts the price someone is willing to pay when you try to sell your business.

If profit, then, is income less expenses, it is important that you get a good grasp of what income and expenses are. These sound like basic terms at first, but quite often there is confusion both in the treatment of items and also the typical 'accountant speak' or terminology.

Types of Income

Income is defined as 'Money received in consideration for exertion, effort or trade of goods.' It can encompass a range of different items. Some common examples are:

- Sales
- Interest and rent received
- Profit on sale of assets or equipment.

You will quite often hear the term 'revenue' used when talking about income. Revenue is again the same concept. Turnover, however, relates purely to the sale of goods or provision of services.

The Urban Myth – Income Versus Capital Injections

When an owner injects money into a business, this is not income. Think of the definition of income. Has there been any exertion or trade of goods? No. The money injected represents a loan from an owner to the business or a form of ownership payment such as shares/units/equity. Monies received in this form are not income in nature and do not relate to the profit-making performance of the business.

Case Study: Understanding Income

Jim ran a successful retail store and needed funds to expand his range of outdoor furniture. He decided that he would put $80,000 that he inherited from his late relative into the business. His bookkeeper coded the $80,000 to income in his accounting software to an account labelled Loan-Jim. This incorrect classification overstated Jim's income as well as his profit. It wasn't until my accounting firm did Jim's year-end tax that he realised the error. Jim spent the best part of 12 months thinking he had made a profit, when this was not the case. This was a significant lost opportunity, as Jim could have addressed his lack of profitability early rather than continuing for months thinking all was well.

COMPONENTS OF A PROFIT AND LOSS STATEMENT

Let's now look at the main components of a profit and loss statement so you have the information you need to analyse yours. Again, if you've been in business for a while you might be tempted to skip this section – I encourage you to read it, though, as there are often important details that even the most experienced of my clients miss.

Trading Account

A trading account is part of a business profit and loss statement. It shows the business's turnover against the direct costs incurred in obtaining that turnover (sometimes referred to as cost of goods sold). Note: we are only interested in turnover when talking about trading accounts. Trading accounts are most common in manufacturing or sales-based industries. Most service industries will not have a trading account and will simply report their turn-over on a basic profit and loss.

Trading accounts allow you to measure what it directly costs to make a sale. It is important to distinguish which costs directly relate to your product or service and which costs are attributed to the running of the business – sometimes termed overheads.

A trading account has three main components:

1. **Sales:** The turnover of your business. This does NOT include other income items such as interest or rent received.
2. **Cost of goods sold:** Represents direct costs related to bringing a product to sale. It's NOT the costs of doing business, but the cost of the thing that is sold. Examples include purchases, materials, direct labour, opening and closing stock.
3. **Gross profit:** The result of sales less cost of goods sold. It represents the profit made at the gross level – before taking into account the rest of the business's income and expenses not directly related to sales.

Table 5.1 shows an example of a trading account for a fictitious business, Bob's Beaut BBQs.

The trading account allows you to see how much money you make on every sale. If your gross profit margin is 50% you are making 50 cents on every $1 sale.

Table 5.1: Trading Account Example

Bob's Beaut BBQs Pty Ltd
Trading Account
For the year ended 30 June 2035

	2035		2034	
	$	%	$	%
Trading income				
Sales	698,589	100	520,685	100
Total trading income	698,589	100	520,685	100
Cost of goods sold				
Add:				
Opening stock on hand	120,000	17	110,400	21
Purchases	562,984	81	374,079	72
	682,984	98	484,479	93
Less:				
Closing stock on hand	180,000	26	120,000	23
Cost of goods sold	502,984	72	364,479	70
Gross profit from trading	195,605	28	156,206	30

Margin Versus Markup

What do you base your prices on – a markup? Or a margin? Many business owners are very often confused by this. **Markup** is setting the price on the basis of cost; it's a percentage of cost. **Margin**, on the other hand, is based on selling price; it's a percentage of selling price.

A 50% markup will result in a product that costs $100 being sold for $150 (see table 5.2).

Table 5.2: 50% Markup

Cost	100	Selling price	150	
Markup 50%	50	Cost	(100)	
Selling price	150	Gross profit	50	50% of cost 33% of selling price

A 50% gross margin means that if a product costs $100 it must be sold at $200 to make a 50% gross margin ($100 is 50% of $200). See table 5.3.

Table 5.3: 50% Gross Margin

Cost	100	Selling price	200	
Markup 100%	100	Cost	(100)	
Selling price	200	Gross margin	100	50% of selling price

In the example of markup (table 5.2), the gross profit is $50 – that is a 33% gross profit margin. This is important to understand because when you talk of profitability and breakeven it's all about sales and percentage of sales. It's very easy to think that by marking up at 50% you're getting 50% of your sales as gross profit – wrong!

What Use is Gross Profit?

Gross profit (sometimes abbreviated GP) is a vital statistic in your business if you are a trading entity. Low gross profit must be combined with high volume to ensure enough profitability to not only cover other expenses but provide owners a return. High-margin operators may have fewer customers, but the process is more intensive in selling.

Low-margin products can be compared to fuel in a service station. High-margin products are the bottle of Coke and choccys in the shop at the service station.

Why does my Gross Profit Change?

Gross profit margins will not only vary between businesses but also within a business. Gross profit will be affected by increases in supplier costs, direct wage increases, changes in levels of wastage or productivity, and discounted sale prices. A business with a decreasing margin will require an increased turnover to compensate. A decreasing margin without a corresponding increase in turnover will result in less gross profit to offset other expenses and lower overall profit for owners. Remember the pricing charts that we referred to in Chapter 4? You can use these to see the huge impact a change in margin can have on your business as well.

Case Study: Sales Vanity

If your sales increased from $1 million to $1.2 million, you would be happy, right?

Yet when I told my client that they were working harder and making less money, I got a confused look of disbelief. Unfortunately, their gross profit margin had deteriorated due to increased supplier costs and reworks/wastage. Their previous gross profit margin of 71% had now dropped to 62%.

They were now making a gross profit of $744,000 – an increase of only $34,000, despite an increase in sales of $200,000. It was hardly worth the extra effort. They were making $18,000 (9%) less on the sales increase. Even more of a concern was the fact that they were earning less on their existing $1 million of sales as well.

By giving the client a much better understanding of their margin, I enabled them to assess their true business performance and take corrective action.

Other Income

This section simply brings together other forms of income not included in turnover, such as interest income, rent received or subsidies for apprentices/trainees. As a rule, anything that is not turnover belongs here. If you do not have a trading account, you will most likely see turnover and other income bunched together under the one income group.

Other Expenses

Many costs in a business are not directly linked to a sale. While some may change with sales volume, they are not direct costs of goods sold. Others are just downright sunk or fixed costs such as rent, insurance and so on.

Remember, with gross profit you are interested in how much money you make from a sale or provision of service. Think of other expenses as the costs of doing business, not as the costs of making the sale.

Everything that does not form part of cost of goods sold will be another expense. But just like income not being the same as money in, an expense is not just money going out. An expense can be an outflow of money that does not have a capital nature. That is, it is used as an instant fix, if you like – a cost that is immediately consumed in the business.

Contrast this to, say, the purchase of a motor vehicle. This is a capital cost as it will be used over time in the business and is not small enough in nature to be deemed consumable. Depreciation is an expense, however. Depreciation is an attempt to recognise the use of the motor vehicle over time and match it against its use in earning income.

Also, money paid to you as the owner, such as drawings, is not an expense. This is a return on your ownership, not money exchanged for goods or effort. Wages is the expense; drawings is the capital equivalent.

Many businesses manage other expenses as a percentage of sales. This allows for easy benchmarks to be set and monitored. For example, consider a business that wishes to spend 5% of turnover on advertising. This is easily calculated as a percentage of sales and monitored over time.

Another good measure for other expenses is against budget. By establishing a comprehensive budget that corresponds to your profit and loss items, you can compare actual to budget and analyse any variances.

Net Profit

Net profit is income less expenses. Gross profit from the trading account flows through to add with other income.

By then deducting your other expenses you are left with a net profit. This is often referred to as the bottom line. It is a measure of the net performance of a business over a period of time. In terms of income and expenses it highlights the excess available for transfer to owners.

Let's now take a look at a profit and loss example for Bob's Beaut BBQs (table 5.4).

Table 5.4: Profit and Loss Example

Bob's Beaut BBQs Pty Ltd
Profit and Loss
For the year ended 30 June 2035

	2035		2034	
	$	%	$	%
Gross profit from trading	195,605		156,206	
Operating expenses				
Accountancy	3,600	0.5	6,500	1.2
Advertising and promotion	1,842	0.3	2,750	0.5
Bank fees and charges	886	0.1	726	0.1
Depreciation	5,310	0.8	7,361	1.4
Electricity and gas	1,178	0.2	1,359	0.3
Freight and cartage	1,680	0.2	1,250	0.2
Insurance	1,985	0.3	7,324	1.4
Interest – Australia	8,600	1.2	9,000	1.7

	2035		2034	
	$	%	$	%
M/V – Fuel and oil	3,596	0.5	4,563	0.9
M/V – Rego/Insurance	5,589	0.8	5,486	1.1
M/V – Repairs	3,678	0.5	4,568	0.9
Printing and stationery	456	0.1	698	0.1
Rent on land and buildings	15,300	2.2	18,125	3.5
Repairs and maintenance	4,466	0.6	5,687	1.1
Superannuation	5,000	0.7	5,800	1.1
Telephone	1,215	0.2	1,352	0.3
Travel, accom and conference	694	0.1	503	0.1
Wages	50,000	7.2	58,000	11.1
Total operating expenses	115,075	16.5	141,052	27.1
Net profit	80,530	11.5	15,154	2.9

Does More Profit mean Better Performance?

Not always. While you may be performing better overall, you have to look at the individual components of the profit and loss in isolation to get a good feel for performance. Net profit is just one measure.

You will most likely see similarities between Table 5.4 and your own profit and loss. Take a moment to review your profit and loss. Can you see any trends? Have any of your expenses increased or decreased significantly in the last year. If so, why? Are any of your expenses a higher than normal percentage of sales? Understanding and being inquisitive about your profit and loss is essential to good financial management.

For example, you may have made a loss for the year. Looking at this in isolation may drive you to despair. However, there may have been issues that caused the loss – for example, an unforeseeable downturn in turnover, a significant increase in supplier costs that could not yet be passed on to the customer, or unmonitored theft by staff affecting gross profit margin. There could also be valid addbacks such as depreciation or voluntary superannuation contributions that distort profit. All of these can be analysed by monitoring individual items and using comparative data.

Profit and Loss Comparisons

How do you improve profit? In Chapter 4 we looked at hidden profits and 'what-if' analysis. When it comes to a more traditional review of financial performance, profit improvement is driven by three main levers:

1. Increasing turnover
2. Being more efficient – increasing margin
3. Keeping costs under control relative to gross profit levels.

It is important, then, to read your trading and profit and loss figures with these three levers in mind, spotting trends as they appear and taking corrective action. For example, sales may be declining. This of itself could be a concern; however, if gross margin is increasing at a rate to maintain a constant gross profit dollar-wise, this could actually mean you are making the same amount of money for less effort. Less effort means more time.

You can also review trends in profit and loss data against benchmarks, budgets and KPIs.

See how the numbers can drive so many facets of your business journey?

UNDERSTANDING YOUR BALANCE SHEET

Most people are familiar with the profit and loss statement. It's the bit that tells you how well you did over the year. It's the bit that supports your income tax return, and as a result, it's the bit your accountant concentrates on when presenting you with your annual figures.

It's the interaction between the profit and loss and the balance sheet, though, that provides a complete picture of your business.

A balance sheet shows your business's financial position **at a point in time**.

It is a picture of your business's financial health and shows you the cumulative effect of your business's operations from the beginning to that point in time.

The balance sheet may look like just a bunch of numbers but once you understand how to read it, and can interpret the story it tells, you can make informed decisions about the direction in which you will take your business and how you will take it there.

Let's have a look at what is in a typical balance sheet (see table 5.5).

Every balance sheet will be structured along these lines, whether your business is operating within a company or a trust, or whether you operate as a sole trader or in partnership with someone else. Every balance sheet will look similar to Bob's, with the same broad headings.

Table 5.5: Example Balance Sheet

Bob's Beaut BBQs Pty Ltd
Detailed Balance Sheet as at 30 June 2035

	2035	2034
CURRENT ASSETS		
Receivables		
Trade debtors	161,544	95,459
Inventories		
Stock on hand	180,000	120,000
Other		
Short term deposits	–	17,000
Total Current assets	**341,544**	**232,459**
NON-CURRENT ASSETS		
Property, plant and equipment		
Plant and equipment – at cost	83,000	53,000
Less: accumulated depreciation	-22,910	-17,600
	60,090	35,400
Total Non-Current assets	**60,090**	**35,400**
Total assets	**401,634**	**267,859**
CURRENT LIABILITIES		
Trade creditors	72,803	49,279
Bank overdrafts	61,540	33,000
Current tax liabilities		
GST	5,250	4,300
Superannuation payable	1,680	1,450
	6,930	5,750
Total Current liabilities	**141,273**	**88,029**

	2035	2034
NON-CURRENT LIABILITIES **Interest-bearing liabilities**		
Bank loans	150,000	150,000
Total Non-Current liabilities	150,000	150,000
Total liabilities	291,273	238,029
Net assets	110,361	29,830
EQUITY **Issued capital**		
Issued and paid up capital	2	2
Retained profits / (accumulated losses)	110,359	29,828
Total Equity	110,361	29,830

We'll now have a look at each of the key headings of the balance sheet – assets, liabilities and equity.

What is an Asset?

Assets are future economic benefits controlled by the entity as a result of past transactions or other events.

That's the technical definition of an asset according to the Australian Accounting Standards Board.

What on earth does that mean?

Basically, an asset is something the business owns.

It could be the cash in your bank account, money owed by your customers, or physical items of plant and equipment.

A current asset is something you own that will be converted to cash within 12 months, making a non-current asset one that has a longer life beyond that.

What is a Liability?

Liabilities are the future sacrifices of economic benefits that the entity is presently obliged to make to other entities as a result of past transactions or other events.

Again, another thrilling technical definition according to the Australian Accounting Standards Board. But what on earth does it mean? Basically, a liability is something your business owes to someone else.

It could be your business overdraft, money you owe your suppliers, or longer-term loans and finance.

A current liability is something you owe that you will have to settle within 12 months, whereas a non-current liability is due beyond that period.

Take a chance now to grab your own financials and look at your own balance sheet. Is there anything in the assets or liabilities section of your balance sheet that you don't understand? If there is, note it down to ask your accountant about next time you catch up.

What are Net Assets?

If assets are what you own, and liabilities are what you owe, then:

*Net assets are what would be left over from your assets
if you paid out all your liabilities.*

Turn back to Bob's balance sheet (table 5.5) and see the 'net assets' line. See how it represents his assets minus his liabilities? Now look at your own balance sheet to see this. Net assets is an important measure as it represents the owner's stake or equity in the business.

What is Equity?

Equity is:

- What you inject into the business – capital contributed – *PLUS*
- Profits the business has made that you haven't drawn out – retained profits – *LESS*
- What you take out of the business – dividends or drawings.

Note: if you operate your business through a company or trust, what you inject into the business and what you've drawn out of the business may be shown as a liability (that is, the company/trust owes you) or an asset (that is, you owe the company/trust). This is because the company or trust is a separate entity to you personally. If you're a sole trader, on the other hand, you *are* your business. There's no legal distinction between the two. A company is a separate legal entity and needs to be treated as something distinct from yourself as the owner of that entity (similarly with a trust).

What you put into the business, plus what your business generates, less what you take out, leaves you with the resources left for your business to continue to operate.

Your equity is reflected in the net assets of the business – that is, the resources your business has to continue to operate.

Equity = Net Assets

OR

Equity = Assets – Liabilities

Now review your own balance sheet. Note that your equity section equals your net assets. What makes up your equity section?

Your business needs assets to operate effectively. That is, it needs plant and equipment, it needs a certain level of stock or inventory, and it needs cash.

Someone has to fund the purchase of these things. Assets are funded by yourself (capital contributions or profits retained in the business – owner's equity) and by other people (liabilities).

What you put in, plus what other people contribute, is used to buy assets. Let's see how this works in practice (see figure 5.1).

Figure 5.1: The Financial Operating Cycle

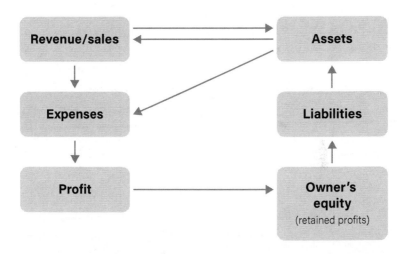

When you start out in business you generally inject your own money to buy some equipment and some stock. You might also borrow some money to do this.

Your capital contribution plus some money from someone else – a liability – is used to purchase assets, being the equipment and stock.

This is represented on the right-hand side of figure 5.1.

Your assets – your plant and equipment and stock – are used to generate sales. Those sales result in more assets, such as accounts receivable or cash.

Your assets, such as cash, are also used to pay expenses.

Your sales, less your expenses, leaves you with profit. That profit, if it is retained in the business, becomes 'retained profits' – forming part of your equity in the business. (Refer to the bottom of figure 5.1.)

Your drawings or your dividends come out of equity. They don't come out of your profit. You've earned the profit – it's part of your equity in your business. If you then choose to draw some of it out, you reduce your equity in the business, which means there are then fewer resources available to generate sales/pay expenses.

If your profits are retained in the business, increasing your equity, they are then used to either purchase more assets (for example, more stock), or to reduce liabilities (for example, repay loans).

And so it goes on – round and round the financial operating cycle.

This cycle is why it is so important to understand your balance sheet as well as your profit and loss. Because your business is not just made up of sales and expenses. Your business's performance is also about efficiency:

- The efficiency with which you convert assets into sales
- The efficiency with which you convert sales into profits
- The efficiency with which you use liabilities and your own equity.

Do you see how the operating cycle is dynamic? It doesn't stop.

The key to your success lies in keeping this financial operating cycle working properly.

Understanding your figures and what they are telling you is an important part of keeping this cycle going properly. However, it's such a dynamic process, you cannot manage the cycle effectively by only looking at your figures (or only part of your figures, such as the profit and loss statement) once a year when you do your tax.

You need to be understanding and interpreting your figures regularly so you can keep your finger on the pulse of your financial operating cycle.

Many business owners manage their business predominantly on the basis of how much cash is in the bank. Have you ever received a surprise when your accountant tells you that you made a profit and will have to pay tax, yet you don't seem to have that much money in the bank? Or alternatively have you received a surprise when your accountant tells you you've made a loss, but you seem to have money available and your sales are growing?

This is very common and happens because cashflow and profit are two very different things. Let's have a look at the differences.

Why is Profit Different to Cash?

Let's go back to what we learned about the profit and loss statement. It shows you how your business has performed over a period of time. It is your income less your expenses.

Cashflow, on the other hand, represents the business's cash inflows less outflows.

Income and expenses, inflows and outflows. Sounds the same, so how can they be so different?

Some examples of things in your profit and loss statement that aren't cashflows are depreciation and interest on loans.

Some examples of things that are cash inflows or cash outflows that don't form part of your profit and loss are debt repayments including tax debt, GST movements and purchase of depreciable assets. Other items include movements in accounts receivable and payable as well as stock on hand.

If these things don't hit your profit and loss statement, where do they appear?

Yes, that's right: **the balance sheet** – making it critical that you understand how to read it, and understand how your profit has been used and why your cash position is the way it is.

We've just looked at the financial operating cycle. You now know that your assets generate your revenue. How efficiently you do that is represented in your profit, and your profit is used to buy more assets, repay borrowings, or distribute to yourself as owner.

Now let's look at another cycle within the financial operating cycle: the working capital cycle (figure 5.2).

Figure 5.2: The Working Capital Cycle

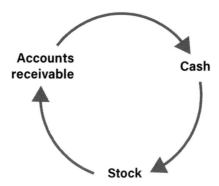

Here's how it works. You spend cash to buy stock, materials or direct labour. If you sell your goods/services on account, a sale results in an account receivable (or debtor). A little while later that account gets paid and you get cash which you use to buy more stock, materials or direct labour, and so it continues.

When your business is growing, this circle gets bigger and bigger. When you're generating more sales, you need more resources to satisfy demand. You then outlay more cash, or extend your overdraft, to pay your suppliers. You hold more stock/work in progress, which you then sell, leading to more accounts receivable, eventually meaning that you end up with more cash coming in the door. The dollars at each point get bigger and bigger.

Sounds great, doesn't it?

And it is great, if the length of time between each part of the cycle is well controlled.

The cycle shows the time lag between outlaying cash to your suppliers and getting cash in from your customers. The time lag consists of the time it takes to move your product off the shelves, and the time it takes your customers to pay.

Even if you are in a service industry and don't hold 'stock' as such, you are likely to have to pay wages for your staff before you bill your customer for the service they provide. The work your staff has done that hasn't been billed yet is your 'stock' or 'work in progress'.

If you are in a retail business part of your circle is closed and you are dealing with only cash and stock. This makes cashflow management much easier, but the circle is still relevant.

So as your business grows and you sell more and more, you need more cash to fund your stock levels. What happens when you get busier and busier making more and more sales? What is it you focus on?

That's right: selling.

If you are not managing your stock levels or your accounts receivable, the time lag will get longer, which means you are out of pocket for longer, and so you need more funding for longer (usually from a lender, for example an overdraft).

If this continues you will run out of cashflow to sustain your operations, and you will grow yourself out of business. Another reason to be understanding and interpreting your balance sheet regularly!

Let's look at this another way, on a timeline (see figure 5.3).

Figure 5.3: Working Capital Timeline – Example A

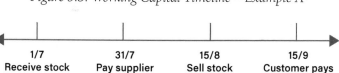

| 1/7 | 31/7 | 15/8 | 15/9 |
| Receive stock | Pay supplier | Sell stock | Customer pays |

It is **46** days between the cash outflow to pay for the stock and the cash inflow from the customer.

Let's consider what happens when it takes you longer to sell and your customer also takes longer to pay (see figure 5.4).

Figure 5.4: Working Capital Timeline – Example B

| 1/7 | 31/7 | 31/8 | 31/10 |
| Receive stock | Pay supplier | Sell stock | Customer pays |

It is now **92** days between the cash outflow to your supplier and the cash inflow from your customer.

That's **46** extra days for which you need to fund that payment to your supplier through an overdraft, a loan or your own funds.

Let's look back and see how Bob's Beaut BBQs looks now that we know about the importance of the balance sheet and cashflow.

Let's look at Bob's trading account (table 5.1, at the beginning of this chapter). Bob's sales increased from $520,685 in 2034 to $698,589 in 2035. That's a 34% increase – pretty good, yes?

Now let's look at his net profit, as listed in his profit and loss statement (table 5.4). His net profit increased from $15,154 to $80,531. This is an increase of more than 430% – fantastic!

If Bob was only monitoring his sales and his profit he'd be laughing.

However, now that we know the importance of the balance sheet and we've looked at some of the differences between cash and profit, let's see what Bob's balance sheet (table 5.5) tells us.

What can you see that might be cause for concern?

You will notice that a lot of Bob's profits are tied up in accounts receivable and stock, with both of those items increasing significantly. Also of concern is that Bob's overdraft facility has blown out, presumably to carry the cashflow cycle as the business grew. Even though Bob's sales are doing great and he's making profits, his cashflow is not so healthy.

This is very common. Many people don't realise they've made profit because cashflow isn't there. They are surprised when they have to pay tax. The cashflow just isn't showing and the surprise is due to lack of monitoring and balance sheet management.

Drawings

Another thing that can greatly impact cashflow is the amount you take out of the business for your own personal use. If you take more cash out of the business than the profit being generated, either your cash reserves will diminish or your debt levels will rise. It's critical to ensure that you manage your business well enough to draw the remuneration you are due for your efforts, as well as ensuring that business funds are not used excessively to fund lavish lifestyle goals well before it can afford to.

Take time now to have a look at your own profit and loss statement and balance sheet. Make note of any observations of profit and cashflow to discuss with your advisor when you next meet.

BREAKEVEN ANALYSIS

Breakeven point is the level of sales volume at which there is no profit and no loss. It's the point at which income exactly covers expenses.

Knowing your breakeven point should be the starting point of developing any budget and it's a key tool in determining whether your pricing is appropriate and/or your costs efficient.

Breakeven analysis helps you work out what level of sales you need to cover your costs. It can also be used to work out what level of sales you need to make a particular amount of profit.

It helps you understand the impact on your business of changes in costs, pricing and volume. You can use breakeven analysis to identify how many extra sales you need to make to cover an increase in costs.

For example, what would happen if your landlord wanted to increase your rent by $5000 per year? How much in extra sales would you need to generate to have the same level of profit with a $5000 increase in rent?

Quite often, when I ask this question, the quick answer thrown back at me is $5000.

Wrong! Let's find out why.

Breakeven analysis revolves around a concept called contribution margin. It's a bit like gross margin, which we covered earlier in the chapter, but is slightly different:

Gross Margin = Sales − Cost of Goods Sold
Contribution Margin = Sales − Variable Costs

Your contribution margin is the amount you have left after **variable costs** are incurred. It's the amount available to cover, or 'contribute' to, your **fixed costs** (see figure 5.5).

Figure 5.5: Breakeven Components

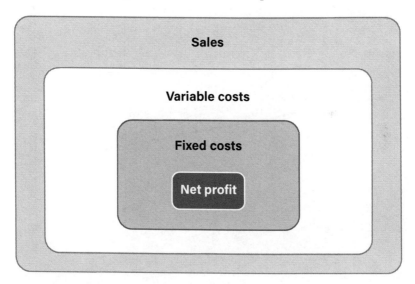

The key to being able to work out your breakeven point is to have a good understanding of your costs. Not only do you need to have an understanding of what your costs are, but you need an understanding of how they behave.

So, what are variable costs and what are fixed costs?

These two terms describe a cost's behaviour:

- **Fixed costs:** Generally, within a reasonable sales range, fixed costs do not vary with sales or production volume. Think items like insurance, rent and administration wages.
- **Variable costs:** Variable costs vary in direct proportion to sales or production volume. If there are no sales, these costs won't be incurred. Think items like stock purchases, contractors and direct labour.

Another way to look at it is: *if a sale doesn't cause a cost, the cost is fixed.*

Be careful – how costs behave, and whether they are fixed or variable, may not be as simple as looking at where your book-keeper puts them in your profit and loss statement. 'Cost of sales' is generally variable and your profit and loss statement will show your gross margin. But some costs may not be cost of sales but still might be variable. Freight and certain promotional expenses can fall into this category.

Let's look at an example (table 5.6).

Table 5.6: Contribution Margin Example

Sales	$1,000,000	100%
Variable costs	($500,000)	50%
Contribution margin	$500,000	50%

In this example, variable costs are 50% of sales and the contribution margin is 50% of sales. This means that for every $1 of sales, 50% or 50 cents is available to 'contribute' to fixed costs. Contribution margin can be expressed as dollars or as a percentage.

You can work out the breakeven point by dividing fixed costs by the contribution margin percentage:

$$\text{Breakeven Sales} = \text{Fixed Costs} \div \text{Contribution Margin Percentage}$$

If fixed costs are $500,000, this business will breakeven at $1,000,000 sales. If fixed costs are more than this, a loss will be incurred. If fixed costs are less, a profit will be generated.

Note there are limitations with this analysis. For example, at some point your sales might increase to the extent that you need to put on another administration assistant or you need to rent larger premises. This will of course increase your fixed costs and your previous breakeven point will no longer hold.

Breakeven analysis, however, can be used to determine what level of sales you would then need to generate to recover that extra salary, rent or other fixed cost.

Who wants to just break even, though? You want to do more than that, don't you? So how do you work out the sales volume you need to make the profit you want?

Simply think of your profit target as an additional fixed cost. It is something that must be covered by your contribution margin. Then:

$$\text{Breakeven Sales} = (\text{Fixed Costs} + \text{Profit}) \div \text{Contribution Margin Percentage}$$

By understanding your average sale value, you can then chunk it down to the number of actual sales you need to make annually, monthly and weekly. These figures are crucial when it comes to formulating your business action plan. In the example above, if the average sale price was $1000, you would need to sell 1000 units to break even.

Pricing and Marketing

You can use this new knowledge to get a feel for what the impact would be if you were to increase your prices.

For example, what would happen if, in the previous example, the selling price per unit was increased from $1000 to $1100 – a 10% increase? How many units would now need to be sold to break even? Let's take a look:

Average selling price per unit: $1100
Variable cost per unit: $500 (no change)
Contribution margin per unit: $600
Fixed costs: $500,000

$500,000 (fixed costs)
÷ $600 (contribution margin per unit)
= 833 units

So, by increasing prices by 10%, you can afford to sell 17% fewer units without worsening your profit position.

You can use the same method to work out how many extra units would need to be sold if you discounted prices but didn't want to worsen your profit position.

Does this look familiar to you? It should. The pricing charts referred to in Chapter 4 are based on this analysis.

Understanding breakeven analysis can do so much more for your business beyond knowing what it takes to just break even. Having this information to hand means you can make informed decisions about pricing and marketing your products.

Controlling Costs

You can also use breakeven analysis to control costs. For example, if you are considering hiring a new salesperson who will cost you $45,000 a year (no commissions, for the sake of simplicity), how much in extra sales need to be generated to cover this person's wage?

$$\$45,000 \text{ (the additional fixed cost)}$$
$$\div 50\% \text{ (contribution margin)} = \$90,000$$

If, by putting this person on, the business is likely to generate more than $90,000 extra sales, then the costs of that person will be covered and the business will be better off.

If the average selling price is $1000 per unit, the new salesperson would need to sell 90 units per year to cover the cost of their wage.

Breakeven analysis will mean you will be making decisions with an understanding of their financial impact on your business.

Calculating your Breakeven Sales Level

Now take some time to look at your own numbers – and calculate your breakeven sales level.

Here's how to do it:

1. Look at your latest profit and loss statement and identify your fixed costs. Mark these with an 'F'.

2. Identify your variable costs. Mark these with a 'V'.
   Note: if you can't decide whether a cost is fixed or variable, be conservative and call it fixed – thus making your breakeven point higher.

3. Add up the total of your fixed costs: $_____

4. Work out your contribution margin:
   Sales: $_____
   less Variable costs: ($_____)
   = Contribution margin: $_____

5. Work out your contribution margin percentage
   (your contribution margin as a percentage of sales) _____%

6. Work out your breakeven point:
   Fixed costs: $_____ (from step 3)
   ÷ Contribution margin: _____% (from step 5)
   = $_____

7. Work out your sales needed to achieve your desired profit:
   (Fixed costs + profit): ($_____ + $_____)
   ÷ Contribution margin: _____% (from step 5)
   = $_____

Now, a couple of exercises for bonus points:

1. If you wanted to spend an extra $5000 on Facebook
   advertising, how much would you need to generate in extra
   sales to recoup that cost?

2. Calculate your contribution margin for the previous year.
   Is it significantly different to the contribution margin you
   calculated above? If so, why? Have you been discounting more
   than usual? Have your suppliers increased their prices? Has
   there been an increase in wastage or a decrease in efficiency?

There are many reasons things can vary; however, unless you're
tracking your contribution margin and are aware of what your

financial figures are telling you, you will not know what to investigate and will not be able to make decisions or take action to correct these things.

GETTING ON TOP OF TAX

Yes, I know. The very mention of that dirty three-letter word makes business owners groan. Normally when tax is mentioned, business owners react adversely; most, in fact, would rather chop off their left arm than pay tax.

Tax, however, is a necessary evil. By minimising tax in an intelligent way, you can reap significant benefits for both yourself and your business. To achieve this, it is important to avoid the rule of thumb that what you don't know won't hurt you. In fact, it's the other way around.

What you don't know WILL hurt you!

If you adopt practices such as not declaring income, falsely claiming deductions or not paying obligations, your business will suffer financially through not only tax office pressure, but on the value that others will see in the figures when you ultimately sell. The less profit you make the less someone will pay for your business.

It has never been more important to have a broad understanding of how your business fits into the tax system. So let's have a look at the broad picture.

Disclaimer: The issues covered in this section are general in nature only. As a result, specific tax advice should be sought from a qualified accountant prior to making any decision based on the content included in this book. No responsibility will be taken for any loss arising out of reliance on information contained within. All information is based on the Australian taxation system. While the concepts may be similar elsewhere, you should research your own country's specific rules.

How are Businesses Taxed?

Businesses are taxed according to the entity they are run through. When you commence business you choose an appropriate entity to trade through. These include individual/sole trader, partnerships, companies and trusts.

Quite often more than one entity is used in a business structure and it is important to understand their interaction for efficient tax planning to occur.

Structures are also used to reduce risk, either to the business or the owner's assets. Companies and trusts, if properly structured, can provide superior risk protection to that provided as a sole trader or partnership. While structuring for risk is beyond the scope of this chapter, you can find a detailed structure comparison table at: **direction.com.au/awesomebookresources**.

Let's now look at the different types of tax structures in more detail.

Individuals/Sole Traders

Individuals pay tax on a sliding scale of rates. Each level or tier is termed a marginal rate. This is important when considering tax planning issues or tax implications of day-to-day transactions such as 'what name should I buy this in?'

Individuals also have liability for other items such as the Medicare levy, and are eligible for various rebates.

By operating as a sole trader, a business is choosing the most simple, inexpensive structure; however, it's leaving the owner open to higher tax rates depending on the taxable profit, as well as possible higher liability risk.

Partnerships

Partnerships are one of the most simple, and most common, structures available. They are inexpensive to set up; however I recommend investing in having a formal partnership agreement established. This helps you avoid any problems on dissolution of a partnership – something that happens all too often.

The most common form of partnership consists of two or more parties who decide to go into business together – normally sharing initial capital funding requirements and skills relating to working in the business.

Partnerships, much like trusts, do not pay tax in their own right.

At the end of the financial year, taxable profit is calculated and distributed to the partners either equally or in accordance with a partnership agreement.

A partner's salary may be paid, as agreed, to recognise the efforts of one partner above another. This will have the effect of skewing the distributions towards one partner in lieu of a partnership agreement.

Once distributed to the partners, the profit is included in their individual tax returns and dealt with accordingly at their applicable rates.

Just like trusts, partners can be either individual or non-individual.

A partnership can distribute a loss. If a partnership incurs a loss, it is distributed to the partners for inclusion in their individual tax return.

Companies

A company is a formal structure that comes into existence by the process of incorporation. Companies are governed by a set of rules contained in the *Corporations Act 2001* and as such are heavily regulated in what they can and can't do. As a result, companies are only entered into when valid reasons exist.

Companies pay a flat rate of tax on their taxable profit. This means that if a company makes $1 of profit, it will pay tax at the current company rate. And if a company makes $100,000 profit, it will pay tax at the same company rate.

The owners of a typical Mum and Dad company are also normally employees and as such, take a wage from the business. Alternatively they are directors and take a directors fee, which is similar to a wage when it comes to taxation.

Superannuation and workers compensation are payable on the owners' wages. Directors' fees will incur these costs if they are paid to 'working' directors of the company.

The ownership interest in a company is a share. It is the same as owning a share in a publicly listed company such as CBA or Telstra. You own a part of a business, and as that business makes a profit, it distributes some of it to you in the form of a dividend.

Assuming that a company has paid tax on its profit, when it pays a dividend it is out of after-tax profits. This is what is known as a franked dividend. Simply put, this means that when you include it in your tax return, tax to the value of the company tax rate has already been paid, and you are not taxed twice.

Loans to directors/shareholders and their associates is another major issue with companies. In 1997 a concept known commonly as Division 7A or debit loans was introduced. As part of this, the tax office put in place legislation that essentially says that if you want to take money out of your business, it has to be in one of three forms:

1. Wages
2. A dividend

3. A loan, formally set up in writing, with a set term and interest, and minimum repayments required.

In practical terms this means that an owner of a company can't draw money out of the business for personal reasons without either treating it as assessable income or borrowing it from the company on commercial terms. The tax office has built in huge disincentives for not complying with these rules.

Case Study: Company Funds Aren't Your Funds

Greg and Sheree came to me from another accountant who had made a mess of their company transactions. Before coming to me, Greg and Sheree decided to help their son and daughter-in-law buy their first house by lending them $50,000. They transferred the money from the company to pay for this. Greg and his (less-than-great) accountant at the time ignored the $50,000 and simply put it on the balance sheet as a loan to Greg and Sheree, with no written agreement. They carried on for a number of years, making no minimum repayments or charging any interest from their company for the loan. As I worked through this issue for them, the ATO could have deemed the full amount of the loan as an unfranked dividend in the year it occurred with potential tax payable by Greg and Sheree being approximately $24,000. Ouch!

Trusts

A trust is a structure that is steeped in tradition and legalese. Given the purpose of this book, I will define a trust in a non-technical way, helping you understand the concept rather than the complexities.

A trust is established with a trustee. Some form of property or operation is placed on trust with the trustee for them to handle as they see fit on behalf of the beneficiaries.

The easiest way to understand trusts is to think of a child's bank account. When you set up a trust account for the child (beneficiary), you (the trustee) have control over what is done with the account and the money. It is the same for business. The trustees hold the business on trust for the beneficiaries.

Now that you understand what a trust is, let's look at some of the essentials.

A trust can be either discretionary or unit-based.

With a discretionary trust, at the end of the year the trustees can decide who to distribute the profits to – they do so at their discretion.

With a unit trust, the profit is distributed in the proportions of the units held. Units are fixed rights, similar in nature to shares.

Tax is not paid directly by a trust unless it elects to retain an amount of profit in its own right. Tax is paid by the beneficiary or unit holder at their relevant tax rate.

Beneficiaries of a trust can be individuals or non-individuals depending on personal preference.

A trust cannot distribute a loss under normal circumstances. Losses are carried forward subject to trust loss requirements and applied against future profits.

Goods and Services Tax (GST) Versus Income Tax

Since the introduction of the GST, businesses have been forced to become directly involved in dealing with tax issues and the tax office regularly. While many businesses now have a reasonable knowledge of how to prepare a business activity statement (BAS), there is still a high level of misunderstanding about how the GST system interacts with the income tax system.

GST is a consumption tax that operates separately and over the top of every transaction in your business. You will note that profit and loss items operate on the net of GST figures.

GST is simply a collection procedure: you charge GST on top of your normal net price, if applicable, and claim back the GST charged on your inputs.

Your GST charged is typically higher than your input tax credits, as many expenses – such as superannuation and wages – don't include GST. Exceptions are businesses such as medical practitioners, whose income is GST free.

A BAS is also normally higher due to other liabilities such as PAYGW (tax witheld on wages) and PAYG instalments (essentially, prepaid tax instalments).

YOUR TAX PLAN

Ensuring that you are on top of your tax obligations is essential for business success. To optimise your tax position, it is necessary to review your business performance part way through the year, allowing tax estimates to be prepared. Those estimates will look at your year to date profit and extrapolate through to the end of the financial year. Once a forecasted profit is determined, tax liabilities can be estimated and options explored to achieve the best tax result. It is too late to implement any strategies to legally optimise your tax, once the financial year has finished. By having a plan in place early, you will also be in a better position to fund any actions arising from your tax planning, without putting strain on cashflow at the last minute.

Tax can be a very daunting area for even the most experienced business owner. By taking a proactive approach, and seeking quality, timely advice, you can not only save tax but also avoid making costly mistakes.

YOUR BUSINESS MONEY PLAN

We have covered a significant amount of ground on the numbers area of your business. You should by now have a good working knowledge of the components of your financials as well as insights into your breakeven and structure position. Armed with that knowledge, you are now ready to bring it all together with your business money plan. Your business money plan focuses solely on the financial side of the business. We will cover the broader business plan in Chapter 6.

Love them or hate them, budgets are an essential part of running a business. There is a universal law that if you earn more than you spend, there will be a surplus left over to apply elsewhere. Think of it like a bucket of water. Your bucket starts out empty. You fill your bucket (sales, debt or invested funds), and take water out over time (expenses, asset purchase or liability reduction). Take too much water out, or not fill the bucket up enough, and you will run dry (go broke). Understanding how much water you need at any point in time allows you to manage how much you fill up or take out.

Just like you need a plan to know how you are going to get to your end point, you need a money plan to understand the financial flows behind your strategy and day-to-day operations. You can then compare your current performance against your money plan, and take corrective action where needed.

So, what is a business money plan and how do you design it?

Start by accessing your downloadable template at **direction. com.au/awesomebookresources**.

Download this resource now and you can complete it as you go through this section of the book.

You will recall that the profit and loss and balance sheet work together as financial documents. Your cashflow is directly tied to both, as any cashflow-related item will impact either the profit and loss or the balance sheet. It therefore makes sense that your money plan takes each report into consideration. This is often called a three-way cashflow. In basic terms, it allows you to design a cashflow forecast that links to both the profit and loss and balance sheet.

The starting point for your money plan is profit and loss. You will lay out your expected sales each month. You will then complete your profit and loss by inputting any other income as well as your expenses. Note that the profit and loss is NOT cashflow. If you operate on an accrual basis, you should be basing your figures on an accrual or as-invoiced basis.

Once you have the profit and loss section completed, it is time to convert this statement to show cashflow on the cashflow forecast sheet. On this sheet you WILL be looking at the cashflow timing of your sales and expenses. In addition you will be adjusting for those items that are 'non cash' yet shown on the profit and loss – for example, depreciation – as well as those that are balance sheet related – for example, asset purchases or loan repayments.

Take note of all of these adjustments, as these form the basis of your balance sheet forecast. As an example, if you borrowed $50,000 from the bank, this will be a cash inflow, and will also increase your liabilities on your balance sheet. It will not hit your profit and loss though.

Do you see how the three documents interact? Don't worry if you are struggling with this concept. Reach out to your advisor, and they will be able to get your money plan up and running with you.

THERE'S AN APP FOR THAT - AUTOMATING YOUR BOOKWORK

As you can see, there's a lot to keep track of when it comes to the numbers in your business. To make sure you can efficiently get it all done, it's important to look at how automation can save some of the hassle.

Many business owners devote too much time to basic bookwork tasks. When I started in accounting, companies kept multiple handwritten ledgers, all feeding into one another in a manual ecosystem that was then used to produce financial reports such as the profit and loss and balance sheet.

While the manual processes have been replaced by sophisticated digital/cloud-based systems, business owners tend to use the bare basics of the tools they have at their disposal. There is always an app for that, but if you're like many business owners you're not getting the most out of the apps you already have.

I don't want to give you an exhaustive list of automation possibilities, but an insight into some simple automation practices that can support you to achieve progress in your business. Once you start automating common tasks, using the tools already at your disposal, you can then extend to an advanced stage.

So, let's take a look at some of the most common bookwork tools that can help you gain efficiencies.

Cloud-Based Accounting Software

While you might already be using software such as Xero, MYOB and QuickBooks, you might not be using the full functionality you have available. Imagine not knowing that your car had an additional gear you could change to. That's right: you would be working the engine harder and going slower. The big-ticket gains here are learning to use bank feeds and bank rules correctly. Teaching your accounting system to remember common transactions minimises data entry. Following on from data entry is the ability to schedule recurring invoices, invoice due reminders and emailed statements to customers owing money. All of these tasks are easily implemented but often ignored. They will eliminate administrative work and speed up customer payments.

Receipt Capture Software

Gone are the days of the good old shoebox. Simply snap a photo of your receipt, upload it and let the software do the rest. With a bit of setup and training, all of those missed expenses, faded receipts and drawers bursting with paperwork are a thing of the past. Trying to backtrack supplier invoices? Easy. Once uploaded into your payables system, a copy is attached to the accounting entry, saving you time when searching for an audit trail of the transaction. You can also ask suppliers to email your receipt-capture provider directly, cutting out yet another step.

Automation Tools

Tools like Zapier or Phantombuster allow you to use the open nature of many software tools to remove double entry. For example, say a prospective customer signs up to your webinar from your website. This can be linked to your webinar platform for registration as well as your CRM system for entry into your nurture email sequence. All of this can be set up to happen automatically rather than the manual process, which looks something like:

Receive registration
> Input to webinar software
> Input to CRM system
> Manually email client (if you remember)

These examples are just the tip of the iceberg. The key is to review your workflows and determine how each task can be done quicker, easier and better by using the automation tools and apps available.

Obviously, tech tool use also has to make financial sense. There is no point investing in an automation app that gets little use or takes longer to manage than the previous way of doing the task. Just because it's now digital doesn't guarantee it's more effective.

Time, then, for you to do a little stocktake and consider what can be automated in your business. Figure 5.6 is an automation stocktake (you can download a digital version from **direction. com.au/awesomebookresources**). To complete the automation stocktake: for each category, list the processes you currently perform in your business; then mark whether you currently complete the process manually, digitally or a mix of both (hybrid).

For example, a process could be entering supplier invoices. If you are doing this manually, it's time to explore how this task could be performed digitally. If you have a hybrid process, it's time to explore how your procedure could become fully automated. And if you're already fully digital, it's time to review your systems' effectiveness and assess whether improvements can be made to streamline.

Figure 5.6: Automation Stocktake

Category	Process	Manual, Digital, Hybrid (M, D, H)	Automation Action
Finance (Think Accounts Payable, Data Processing)			
Marketing (Think Social Media Posting, Content Creation)			
Admin (Think Letters, Email, Appointments)			
Operations (Think Production Efficiency, Delivery)			
Customers (Think Communications, Meetings, Follow-Up)			
Your People (Think HR, Safety, Office Environment)			
You (Think Time Management, Organisation, Scheduling)			

This process really can bring about fundamental change in your business. While we have focused on automation of your bookwork and administration, think outside the square to your operations. What processes could be refined or automated to increase productivity and remove friction within your business?

SUMMARY

Being in control of your numbers is essential for business financial success. Ignore your key numbers at your own peril. In fact, the integration between your business and your life means that not being on top of your business numbers results in not being on top of your personal life.

Key to understanding your numbers is having the knowledge of how to read your profit and loss statement and balance sheet. These documents provide the information you need for strategic decision-making for your business. The profit and loss provides detail on your gross profit margin, allowing breakeven analysis and benchmarking of key drivers. The balance sheet provides your business's net worth. You can draw key ratios from its contents, providing key information regarding stock and accounts receivable management.

From these two documents comes the ability to understand your cashflow cycle, as well as build your detailed money plan to follow as you move through the next 12 months. By monitoring cashflow, you will be able to take necessary action, ensuring the numbers work for you, rather than against you.

Business structure and tax are foreign concepts to many business owners. Your structure may have been set up by a well-meaning advisor, without you really understanding how it works or why a particular structure was chosen. By understanding structures more deeply you can have more sophisticated discussions with your advisors when discussing structure options.

Behind any great numbers system is a wealth of data entry and administrative tasks. These often cause stress and excessive time to complete. No business owner has said they enjoy the red tape and administration involved in doing business. Modern systems allow significant automation of what were once cumbersome, tedious manual processes. By linking various systems together using open software technology, and making the best use of apps, you can eliminate much of the double handling and automate previously manual tasks.

Your aim is not to become an accountant (god forbid) but to feel in control of your numbers and become financially secure.

As the enabler of your awesome life, your business needs to be financially sound. Being on top of the numbers allows you to not only be aware of business performance, but make better business decisions. Better business decisions significantly impact your ability to create the lifestyle you desire.

CHAPTER 6

PLANNING

I love travel. When I travel, I like to explore a little. I'm not a tour bus kind of guy. Give me a hire car, a GPS or a map and a bit of background research on where I want to go and I'm there. Well, okay, when I say a *bit* of background research, I mean a hell of a lot of research. You see, while I don't want to take the clinical tourist-trap route, it simply doesn't make sense to me anymore to just travel aimlessly.

I once travelled to Italy, staying near a small Tuscan village called Torrita di Siena, as part of a European holiday. I booked accommodation and arranged a hire car but did very little else in terms of planning. I was too busy at the time with work, and figured I'd just get there and work it out as it happened. Big mistake.

After arriving the night before, I sat next to a couple at breakfast the next morning. They asked, 'Did you go to the Palio yesterday?' I replied unwittingly, 'Um, no... what is the Palio?' Turns out the Palio is Siena's biggest annual event. It's an age-old horse race where the participants dress in traditional costume and race around a cobblestone square covered in dirt for the day. It was the equivalent of arriving in Madrid the day AFTER the running of the bulls.

On the same trip, I was again uninformed and freewheeling it south from Barcelona, expecting to stop in along the coast at Valencia, find a hotel and enjoy another part of Spain. On arriving in Valencia, I was greeted by lines of traffic and detours bypassing the main city centre. 'El Papa, El Papa!' laughed the fuel attendant hysterically, as I asked for directions. Turns out the Pope (El Papa) himself was in town that day. My chances of accommodation any-where within two hours was zero, resulting in a long drive further south to Alicante.

Moral of the story: be prepared, do your research. Have contingency plans and don't rely on what others say. Get the plan down and follow it, as it will save you time, stress and money – and you may just get to where you should (or want) to be.

In this chapter, we are going to look at how you can take that plan you say you have in your head, and turn it into an actionable powerhouse that will take your business to where you want to go, and beyond. We will look at the importance of getting your team involved and how to chunk things down into manageable parts.

An essential part of your planning should also involve thinking about protecting what you are building. This involves protecting your business as well as the wealth you will be creating as part of your journey. While asset protection is a complex and detailed area, I will frame it in easy-to-understand terms and provide a basic framework to consider when seeking more complex advice.

GETTING YOUR PLAN OUT OF YOUR HEAD

You're probably saying, 'I don't need a business plan because my business is doing okay.' Stop telling yourself lies! Research published in the *Journal of Management Studies* revealed that companies that plan grow 30% faster than those that don't.

The problem might be that you've only heard about academic-type business plans. Those are rubbish! They're basically waffle with headings. The type of business plan I support is a business action plan. It provides the framework for strategic long-term planning, as well as setting out the most important part of the plan, the actual actions required to implement the strategy. It's a dynamic plan that changes over time as your business grows.

Business plans have a common benefit regardless of the entrepreneur: **clarity**. I like to think of a business plan as the GPS for your business. It helps you set your destination and recalculate when things start to veer off track.

Clarity and targets help you create contingency plans. The future can be obscure, but you can still have contingency plans in place for when things don't go exactly the way you'd hoped.

'I don't need a plan, it's all in my head. And that's where I want to keep it.' Well, that's great. However, how many other things are going on in your brain each second, minute or hour?

I like to describe it like this: there's front of mind and there's the subconscious. You have your plan at the front of your mind, then something else jumps in there. That other thing is going to kick your business plan into your subconscious (or the back of your mind). Your plan has now become reactive instead of proactive.

A great business plan isn't a reactive document. Instead, it's a proactive document that you use for business success. How are you going to keep up with what's happening with your business plan if other thoughts keep coming in and kicking it out?

Keeping your business plan in your head leads to a never-ending cycle of frustration and exhaustion that takes you nowhere.

There's no point making a restrictive plan, either. Business owners often ask me if they can just use a template. There are three problems with business plan templates:

1. They limit input from multiple people
2. You're restricted to the prescribed format
3. They often follow an academic model that gets little results.

You're free to use templates, but will those templates give you the results you seek? I could give you a template with this book, laying out the way I write business plans, and you could use it if you like. However, your plan will come up short because you haven't included the expertise needed in that planning process.

Business plans change over time, and that's life. Things happen. You can't expect everything to work out exactly the way you predicted. That's why your business plan needs built-in flexibility. So, if you need to change your plan because something happened, then you change it. Don't sit there and say, 'Oh, I'm not going to do a plan because things will change. We'll get six months through it and things will be totally different.'

So change the damn thing! Don't *not* create a plan because you think things are going to change.

BRINGING THE PLAN TOGETHER

At the heart of any great plan is a strengths, weaknesses, opportunities and threats (SWOT) analysis. You might be tempted to dismiss the idea of SWOT analysis thinking it's a cliched process. However, what you need to realise about a SWOT analysis is the power that it has within your business planning process.

A SWOT analysis is there to help you look at four key areas in your business before you start any planning around objectives, strategies and actions:

- **Strengths:** Things that you're good at, that you excel at, that you really want to amplify in your business.
- **Weaknesses:** Things that you're bad at, that you avoid thinking about, that you can improve. They might be processes or systems – all of those things that you're not getting to, or you feel are not your strong suits.
- **Opportunities:** Things that your business could take up or introduce as part of a growth or improvement strategy. It could be a new market, product or acquisition.
- **Threats:** Things you need to mitigate in your business. Things that may never eventuate, but if you are not considering them, you are inviting risk into your business. Remember: less risk, more value.

Strengths and weaknesses are often referred to as internal factors – things that are completely within your control. Opportunities and threats can be seen as external, meaning that they are heavily influenced by dynamics beyond you and your business.

An active SWOT analysis lays the foundation for your plan. Let's now look at each element and determine what you need to be looking at in your business, so you can start to put in those building blocks for your business plan.

Strengths

Strengths are those things that you are really good at; the things that set you apart from your competition; the things that make you a desirable object for your customers or your clients. Those strengths can't be wishy-washy, though. Many business owners that I work with initially list generic strengths like:

- 'We're good at what we do'
- 'We are nice'
- 'We care'
- 'We've been around for 25 years'
- 'We have a whole heap of letters after our name'
- 'We're very, very skillful'
- 'We're the best in the business.'

None of that means anything. Instead, you're looking for specifics.

Let's say, for instance, you're a signwriter and your strength is in a particular style of sign or a particular product that you can produce. It might be a 3D sign. It might be something that is backlit. It could be jobs that are in hard-to-reach spaces. Think about what your unique strengths are in your business. If you are a business that says, 'We care', look at that strength a little differently. What is it about caring that matters to your customers or your clients? Is it your after-sales service? How can you explain that as a unique strength rather than just a generic statement such as, 'We care about our customers'? I'd like to hope that most businesses care about their customers. You wouldn't advertise, 'We couldn't care less about our customers', would you?

Think a bit deeper as to what your true strength is. Then, once you understand what that true strength is, the trick with the SWOT analysis is to say what is it that you're going to do with this strength to make sure that you capitalise on it. If you're the signwriter who specialises in signs installed at great heights or in really hard-to-reach places, or you produce a unique type of product, what's your market for that? How are you going to communicate the strength that you have over and above your competition?

How are you going to tell your customer about that strength? If it's your after-sales service that sets you apart, how can you build that into your product offering? It's all about amplifying your strengths.

Personally, I like to think my strength is my ability to communicate information in an easy-to-understand way. My business tagline is: *Easy to deal with, easy to understand*. At each and every meeting or client communication we try to take away the lingo, take away the jargon, and communicate the information in a way that is easy to understand. We have this in our own SWOT analysis, and we capitalise on it each and every time we interact with a client to make sure that we're living by that strength. It means we're taking advantage of what attracts clients to come and deal with our business.

Weaknesses

The important part about weaknesses is the ability to put your hand up and recognise the things that you aren't that good at. It's important to understand this in your business, because weaknesses are the things that you're going to need to aim to improve. There's no point putting your head in the sand and believing that you're the greatest if the evidence says otherwise. You need to recognise that there are things that aren't right in your business, and that need to change.

'Concentrate on the one percenters' is a common phrase. That means making 1% improvements on a whole range of different things. Again, just like strengths, don't go for a statement so broad it loses meaning. Don't say, 'I'm not very good at administration.' It doesn't mean a lot. You can dig deeper into that. Is it the financial side of administration that challenges you? Is it the actual processing of too much red tape? What is it that you particularly struggle with?

Your weakness might be that you're slow to turn around jobs. It might be that you are poor at customer service and you don't like dealing with people. You need to recognise things such as these as possible weaknesses for you in your business. You may need to recruit people who can be customer-facing, while you focus on the technical side of the business. To manage weaknesses, first of all you must recognise them, then dig deeper into what they are, and then look at strategies to improve.

Your weakness might be lead generation. If your lead generation is weak, look at what the leading indicators are. Are you networking in your business? Are you actually expanding your sphere of influence? Are you keeping some form of CRM system or a customer database to be able to continue to nurture those people that you come into contact with? A lot of business owners simply say, 'We are struggling to get customers.' They wonder why, yet they've got no lead generation or customer process in place. It's therefore critical to look at what the weakness is, look at the reasons why, and then, and only then, can you start improving it.

Once you know the causes of your weaknesses, it's not just a simple case of fixing them. Trying to get a business owner to change is a large part of the battle. The objectives and the strategies that come out of looking at your weaknesses are very important as part of your overall business action plan. Having clear actions helps ensure change management flows smoothly, objectives are achieved and weaknesses resolved.

Opportunities

This part of the SWOT analysis requires deep thought. You need to look at the opportunities that are out there for your business. It all starts with discovery.

It's time to go into the thinking room and start to pull apart your business, what you do and what other opportunities are out there for you that you could take advantage of. Once you've determined the potential opportunities, you need to look at their viability. Start to pick them apart, as not every opportunity is worthwhile. This is an important step, as you could spend a lot of time, resources and money chasing something that just isn't going to be profitable. Sure, you can do it, but it doesn't mean that you're going to make a profit. That's very important. I once said to my team, 'We can sell fish and chips in the reception area if we want to, but is it going to make us money?'

Once you determine which opportunities are viable, start to put cases around them and how you are actually going to take up the opportunity. How are you actually going to implement the objectives and the strategies in and around that opportunity? That's when it falls into place as part of your business action plan.

Threats

Threats can come from all sorts of different places. Covid-19 was an extreme example of a threat. Businesses were basically blindsided. However, threats are in existence in business every single day, whether there's a pandemic or not. They're often things that shouldn't be ignored or put in the corner, or the back of your mind.

Many business owners don't think about threats, as it feels negative. Positivity is great, but you need to be realistic. And the fact is, if your nightmare competitor sets up next door tomorrow and wipes you off the map, that's a threat that is best to consider early.

It doesn't need to be a competitor, either. It could be something that's economically based. Perhaps it's something that you could never imagine, so you simply need to look at risk protection.

It could be something you know exists and you're just waiting for it to happen. You need to mitigate these threats.

Identifying threats means you're recognising potential issues, you're pulling your head out of the sand and you're saying, 'What negative impact could this have on my business? What could happen if my nightmare competitor set up next door? What could happen to this business if I'm run over by a bus tomorrow? What could happen to this business if somebody sues us for something that we did? What could happen to this business if one of our suppliers ceased trading or there was a shortage of supply? What could happen to this business if the one client that makes up 80% of our revenue all of a sudden goes bust, or decides to use one of our competitors?' There's a whole range of threats that need to be looked at and mitigated. It's a very important part of any business plan.

None of us is bulletproof. We all have our kryptonite.

Think about the threats to your business, and then start to work on those. Think about what would happen to your business if your threat did occur, and how you might mitigate that. What could you put in place to make sure that you avoid or minimise the risk of it occurring?

Lose the Motherhood Statements

Once you have completed your SWOT analysis, there are a few more key areas to work on in bringing your plan together. The first is losing the motherhood statements: those pithy, feel-good declarations that many business owners feel compelled to include in their business plans.

This may be a controversial viewpoint, but Simon Sinek's concept of identifying your 'why' doesn't belong in a kickass business plan. It's great to understand your 'why' and let that purpose infiltrate your business. But it does **not** belong in your business action plan.

A kickass business plan should look at objectives, strategies and actions. I don't sit down for half the day trying to help my clients understand their 'why'. Instead, we look at:

- What's happening in their business
- What they are trying to achieve
- How they are going to achieve it.

The academic-style business plan with a mission and vision is a bag of rubbish. Knowing your 'why' doesn't mean you're going to achieve or implement anything in your business.

Set Clear Objectives

A business plan should lead to clear actions. Business plan objectives should follow the SMART goals principle (specific, measurable, achievable, relevant and timebound) for each area within your business:

- Marketing
- Operations
- Finance
- Product
- People.

Each area will have different objectives. An example of a great objective is:

Create a sales division within the company, separate to the efforts of the directors, by the end of March 203X.

Create Strong Strategies

Strong strategies clearly outline what you're going to do to achieve your objectives. They answer one question: how? The objectives are the *what* and the strategies are the *how*. You should have a strategy for each objective. An example of a great strategy is:

> *Employ two sales staff, each responsible for budgets of $300,000 in sales.*

Act on Strategies

Next, answer these questions:

- What has to happen to implement the strategies?
- Who's going to do it?
- When are they going to do it?

These answers then help you group actions into blocks. It's important to hold your team and yourself accountable for each action. Before you hold people accountable, though, you need to get them involved.

GETTING YOUR TEAM ON BOARD

There is no point having a plan that only you know about. Likewise, there is no point having a plan that does not get implemented. It's the old saying: a plan without action is a wish.

So when should you involve your team and how do you do it effectively? I recommend bringing your team in at the SWOT analysis stage. Now before you start to shudder at revealing all your dirty laundry in front of your team members, don't worry; the best way to approach this is to have a team SWOT session *before* you go through the exercise yourself.

When you're putting yourself out there in front of your staff, you need to ensure that you have a willingness to listen and a thick skin to any criticism you may not agree with. Asking your team members, those at the coalface, for their opinions not only gives you great input for your business plan process, but also supports an inclusive environment that motivates your team members when the plan is rolled out. They'll have a sense of ownership when they know they have been listened to.

Once the plan is ready, you will need to assign actions to team members. Remember, the plan is not just for you to implement – you simply can't do it all by yourself. In assigning actions to team members, you are giving them responsibility and empowering them to make key decisions that affect the business as a whole. If you provide them with the structure and support needed, they will flourish in getting things done, and your business will be greater for it.

If issues raised by the team don't make the plan, explain why, with clear reasons. If your team encounters difficulties during implementation, jump in and help them get it done. This style of leadership will create significant loyalty from your team, particularly in regards to achieving the plan.

Case Study: The Team Knows Stuff

Keith ran an independent grocery store. As part of his business development, we ran a strategic planning day with him and his wife to formulate a growth path for the next one to three years. Part of the process was a mystery shop the day before, as well as a session with Keith's team on the morning after the strategic planning day. The morning after was a Saturday, and Keith's team consisted of five 16- to 18-year-olds – a tough gig.

> As his team members walked in, bleary eyed and seemingly disinterested, we all thought *what a waste of time this is going to be*. But our initial impressions couldn't have been further from the truth. Each and every team member contributed pure gold that day. We covered everything from strategies to deal with waste, to shop fitout and rostering. We did more strategy with the team than we did with Keith and his wife the day before.
>
> Your team members know things you will not. They also have the answers that you don't.

CHUNKING IT DOWN

The typical business action plan will cover 12 months. While it's common to do so, you don't need to align your plan with a financial or calendar year. It doesn't matter when you start, it just matters that you do. What is important is the 'chunking down' of the plan into smaller parts. These parts start with the dates or periods where you will perform shorter implementation bursts, or 'sprints' (typically quarterly), as well as chunking down the big numbers or tasks into small, achievable parts. By doing this, you allow yourself to achieve wins regularly, which builds momentum. You also can see the reality in any targets you may set.

Take for example a common objective of increasing sales by a particular dollar figure by a particular date. Let's say next quarter you want to increase quarterly sales by $200,000 compared to last year. Sounds pretty standard, doesn't it? However, this objective lacks any real sense of reality. You can't immediately picture what a $200,000 increase in sales means. By using chunking, you can change that. Firstly, there are 13 weeks in the quarter; that means you need to find an extra $15,000 in sales per week. Given your average sale is $3000, this means that you need an extra five sales per week to make it happen. If you know that an average of two out of three enquiries lead to sales, this means you need to do seven to eight extra quotes per week to get there. Now, think even harder. Where will you find those extra customers to quote, and is the target achievable? What action steps need to happen, by when, to make it work? By chunking down your objectives, you bring your plan to life, ensuring it aligns with tasks you know you can do.

Quarters seem to be the most common and effective period to chunk your plan down to. Ninety days provides an optimum time to achieve tasks and also keep focus. Any shorter, and the sprint is over before you start. Longer, and you will either tire of the exercise or reduce your intensity to fit the longer time period.

So, if you chunk it down to four quarters in a plan, how do you decide what to prioritise in which quarter?

The use of themes is an efficient way of garnering focus for each sprint. While there will always be continuing or isolated parts of your sprint, you will see common threads run through your overall plan. Themes such as growth, processes, production and focus could all be used as an overarching focus for the quarter. You then implement strategies based on each quarter's theme.

An alternative to this is to look at what the biggest, most pressing issues are in your overall plan. These big-ticket items then take priority in each 90-day sprint. The issue I have with this method is that you may become discouraged with your progress and start to wander, eventually pushing the big task into the next 90-day period – and so begins the road to not really achieving anything at all.

Laser focus comes from having a clearly defined plan, with action items allocated to team members, and those actions implemented over a defined period of time. This is the essence of chunking down.

A 90-day sprint, well designed and themed, will provide significant buy-in, improve performance and ensure actions are completed. A well-designed 90-day plan also provides a massive accountability structure for you and your coach (if you have one).

Visit **direction.com.au/awesomebookresources** for a downloadable 90-day sprint format that we use in the Vector Business Platform.

Take some time to download and review the template in the context of the bigger plan that you create from this chapter. Try to make your actions align with realistic, achievable and chunked-down targets. You will find your ability to focus, and the momentum gained from actioning tasks, will change the way you have previously looked at plans in your business.

PROTECTING WHAT YOU'VE BUILT

You can spend a lifetime in business. Think again about your purpose in business. A business creates an income and an asset that grows in value. This increase in business wealth will most likely allow you to build wealth in other areas of your life – perhaps property, shares or other forms of investment. It can also allow you to build an awesome lifestyle.

Business can also present significant risk. In Chapter 3 I introduced the concept of risk and how it affects your business value. Now, let's take a look at the types of risk that affect asset protection, which are commonly classed as either personal risk or financial risk.

Personal Risk

We would all love to think that our business can operate without us, but for most of us this simply is not the case. You might be tightly linked to the operations of the business, or financially the business might be so closely tied to you that you are the only one willing to play a part in it.

But why does that matter?

Let's say you wake one morning and it's a usual day. You make yourself a coffee, jump in the shower still half asleep, and get ready for the day ahead. As you leave the house, you kiss your spouse goodbye, pat the dogs, start the car and drive off to work. But today is not a usual day, is it? Today is the day that your fate is handed to you.

Perhaps that routine doctor's appointment turns out to be not so routine.

Perhaps you are involved in a fatal accident on your way to work.

Perhaps something happens at work that makes you decide that the strain of business is all too much, and you decide to look for a way out.

Perhaps you return home to find your loved ones have left, and that's all they wrote.

No matter what your 'perhaps', fact is, your personal life and business life has changed in an instant. There was no way of you predicting that this would happen. But happen it did. And now is when most business owners finally consider what they should have all along. How do I protect what I have created? How do I ensure that the wealth that has been built is not destroyed as a result of events outside of my control?

The first way to protect yourself against personal risk is considering your business's structure (I introduced structure in Chapter 3). Ensuring that you have square pegs in square holes and the right structure allows you to shield your assets from any detriment befalling you.

Take, for example, a company. Many small business owners establish a company as a Mum and Dad business, with 50% ownership each (this is called a joint shareholding). Often the advice they receive around structure is inadequate, and in addition to joint shareholding, Mum and Dad end up both being directors. This opens up significant legal exposure within the entity. Consider a builder who has their non-working spouse as a company director. Any legal action taken against the company would affect *both* husband and wife, despite the fact that only one of them is actively involved in the day-to-day operations. This can put at risk assets that could be otherwise protected in the name of the non-working spouse.

Lack of consideration for the following issues is bound to end in long-term pain:

- People in high-risk industries (such as medical, professional and construction) holding ownership
- Lack of shareholder/partnership agreement – a rulebook in case the worst happens
- Lack of cross-insurance of shareholders, in particular third parties
- No wills, powers of attorney or enduring guardianships considered.

Often structures are put in place purely as vehicles for tax without any consideration to individuals' risk. Complex advice should be sought when pursuing asset protection.

Financial Risk

No one operates a business thinking that it will end up in financial difficulty. Reality is, though, that many business owners arrive at a point where they need to seek professional insolvency assistance. At this time, having a smart structure designed to ensure that otherwise good assets aren't exposed to business financial difficulty and vice versa is critical.

To organise your affairs in such a way you should consider:

- Structure
- Asset ownership
- Licencing issues within your business
- Structure of debt and security given
- Management of any administration matters.

Ignoring financial risk is quite common. When financial difficulty hits, and it combines with lack of preparation, business owners often bury their head – which only exacerbates the problem. This has massive impacts on the business, the individual stakeholders as well as the owner's mental wellbeing. Do not take this area lightly or put it off until you have the time. Act now – it's the ultimate insurance policy for your business.

SUMMARY

The motto 'be prepared' has served the Scouting movement well for over a century. The same motto can also serve your business and personal life. Being prepared by having a plan in place, and following it, forms the centrepiece of any great business development journey.

A great plan needs to be flexible as things will change. The common resistance to planning, due to the fact that things may change or that you have it all in your head, is a falsehood. Change is inevitable, and to not plan because of something that is a constant is a cop-out. Maybe you don't want to plan because you don't want change to happen? Keeping everything in your head just results in inaction, ensuring you don't have to face change. As a new bright shiny object enters your mind, the old plan gets shunted to the back, and you end up with so many things spinning around up there that you don't know which way to turn.

At the heart of any great plan is the concept of objectives, strategies and actions. To determine which objectives to target, you need to conduct a robust SWOT analysis, reviewing your strengths, weaknesses, opportunities and threats. Your objectives should focus on amplifying strengths, improving weaknesses, taking advantage of opportunities and mitigating threats.

By bringing your team on board, you are not only inviting input from the coalface but also ensuring others have buy-in to the plans of the organisation, building a strong culture of account-ability and loyalty.

Chunking down the plan into 90-day sprints, preferably themed, as well as chunking down the components into targets that actually mean something, will allow you to align your actions with the targets and hit them regularly.

Planning is critical for getting clarity on where your business is heading. Just as important is the need to plan to protect what you have built. You can't just build the house, you must protect it and insure it against those wishing to destroy it.

Once again, how could you possibly keep all of this in your head? Is it any wonder that most business owners flail around aimlessly and never address the key issues until it is too late? The ONLY way to alleviate issues is to plan well and implement your actions. Your business will flourish, you will have complete clarity over where you are heading and what needs to be done to get there, and your personal life will be far more relaxed than the alternative.

CHAPTER 7

IMPROVEMENT

Throughout this book we have considered the tools that will help you assess your current business performance. Whether it be gaining awareness through business valuation, hidden profit and needs analysis, or understanding your numbers through regular monitoring of key ratios, or the SWOT analysis and team involvement as part of your business plan, these are all areas where you are identifying things that can be improved in your business. Improvement requires change, often BIG change, and if I know one thing about humans it's that we do everything to avoid change. Change management is a constant tussle with what you feel comfortable with. You may have run your business a certain way for many years. However, to make real progress, change is required.

The constant nature of change means that your business is always improving. If you aren't moving, you will get run over – there's nothing more certain. Maintaining improvement is tough, and it's why I often talk about small changes – often referred to as one percenters. You don't have to change things monumentally. In fact, that is often the worst thing you can do. It works against human nature. Change things inch by inch and no one will really notice. If you are a great leader, your team will actually *lead* the charge.

As you embark on your improvement journey, ensure that you are documenting your processes. Business improvement is a great way to revisit old systems, if you have them, or create new ones. This focus on documenting your way of doing things doesn't only improve operations but is another way of reducing risk and in turn increasing value in your business.

Now, before we get into the specifics of improving your business, it's time to check in on your fears. Don't hide it – it's natural to not want to change. However, stick with the process. You want to look at what needs improving and take note of what works, what doesn't and adjust. Then rinse and repeat. Improvement is constant – that's why you will spend three quarters of the next 12 months in this space, oscillating between it and Accountability. So don't fear it, lean in and let's start improving your business.

YOUR WAY OR THE HIGHWAY – SYSTEMS AND PROCEDURES

A great business has a consistent way of doing things: a set of procedures that everyone involved adheres to. The procedures support the business plan, as well as the vision and culture of the organisation. A business devoid of procedures and systems is reinventing every time it does something.

Those who are resistant to documenting procedures are typically the same people who are resistant to business plans. They think that they have everything in their heads and don't need the restriction and inflexibility of one way of doing things. Imagine if you boarded a flight and overheard the pilot saying to their co-pilot, 'Look, don't waste time doing all that precheck stuff, I've flown this plane a thousand times, we'll be right.' It wouldn't fill you with a great deal of confidence, would it?

McDonald's is the golden (see what I did there) child of procedures and systems. The business is able to rely on a youthful workforce performing tasks well beyond their years. How do they do it? No matter where you go, the product is the same. Sure, there is variation of menu, and also quality occasionally, yet you generally know what you are going to get. You arrive at a drive-through, you know the drill. It's mechanical, but it works. What happens, though, if it is too mechanical? It's simple: make the task so mechanical and automatic so that you actually have the time to add the golden (there I go again) touches.

For another example of mechanics, let's look at an old-school vending machine. You put your money in, you type a code, the arm reaches up to your chosen product, the product proceeds to the chute, and the machine gives you your change. Not a human in sight. The vending machine is an archaic example of a programmed system. In this era of artificial intelligence, so many more advanced things follow a logical structure. Remember: get the consistency from the system, and add the golden moments beyond that.

So let's think about your business for a second. How many different tasks are done in your business every day? Of those tasks, how many are likely to be performed again? Of those tasks, how many have you created a system or process for?

A really simple way to gauge how systemised your business is is to keep a log of the tasks you do each day, and then in that log, cross out anything that is so unique that it will NEVER occur again. Everything else needs a procedure.

What, then, do procedures and systems look like, and how do you go about designing them?

A system is defined as a set of principles or procedures. A system is the combination of a number of methods grouped together to produce a result. A procedure on the other hand is a single method or way of doing something. As an example, in a business there may be a payroll processing system, which comprises many different procedures for each task that needs to be performed.

There are essentially two ways to approach designing your systems and procedures:

1. **Inside-out approach:** This approach requires you to keep track of those tasks that are recurring and build your procedures around those. Bit by bit you will build out your procedures, which are then grouped inside out into your systems for each area of your business.

2. **Top-down approach:** A more structured and complete method is to create systems for the key areas of your business and work your way down into subsystems and procedures. The key areas in your business are the same as those that you encountered when creating your business plan. You may have additional categories, but the typical ones are:

   - Operations
   - Finance
   - Marketing
   - People
   - Product.

Now, underneath each of these categories come your systems and subsystems. Under finance, for instance, will come payroll, and under payroll will come the procedures required to allow the payroll function to be fulfilled, such as timesheet completion, award interpretation, rostering, processing, leave management and so on.

You can see that the top-down approach, while more formal, allows you to analyse your business in a much more structured way than simply what comes up at the time. Inside-out is great for refining tasks or adding new procedures when they occur.

Systems lend themselves to flowcharts, swim lanes and diagrammatical presentation. Procedures can be flowcharted in part, but will quite often be in a written format, checklisted and in some cases signposted.

Figure 7.1 is an example of a procedure template. The key is to have something that works for you that can be produced in a consistent format. Keeping these digitally and controlling your versions will ensure the latest systems are always in use.

Figure 7.1: Procedure Template Example

Executive Assistant

Document ID: MKTG0010

Flowchart link: https://yourprocedures.com.au/MKTG0010

Overview: Update CRM for Customer/Prospect Changes/Additions and Deletions.

Responsibility	Steps	Links
Executive Assistant	1. Enter New Prospects Software	
	2. Ensure New Prospect is Added to Appropriate Sequence	CRM Sequence Guide
	3. Check for any Contact Updates and Processes Where Relevant	Client Update Register
Sales Manager	4. Authorise Contact Deletions	Deletion Checklist
Executive Assistant	5. Delete Contact in Software	

MANAGING CHANGE

I love doing change work with business owners. The impact an expert advisor can have in helping a business owner move from an undesirable position to feeling enthused and passionate about what they do is significant. Yet the process is not easy. So many issues get caught up in change management. It could be the team that is resistant to change, or perhaps it's the customers who are resistant. Or it could be the owner, the very person who wants and needs the change, that resists it with every fibre in their body. Quite often, if I challenge owner resistance I'm met with a whole raft of excuses and denial. All of these factors make change work a sensitive area of business improvement. We can identify the improvement areas – that's the easy part. Getting actions implemented, though, takes time, focus and a large dose of psychology.

Most people resist change due to fear. Fear of failure. Fear of criticism. And in some cases, a fear of success (we'll get to that one a little later). It stands to reason then that if you can address your fear of change, you will be able to change your business in a positive and timely manner.

Fear of Failure

Every decision contains a risk. Your job is to understand that risk and make an educated decision as to whether the risk is worth the result. What's the worst that can happen? A great accountability partner will help you here. 'We can't do that,' you may say. My question to you is not 'Why?' My question is, 'What if you *could* do it? What would that need to look like? How would you feel if you could achieve that? Tell me what's happening in that moment.' It's part visualisation, part realisation.

Fear of Criticism

If your personality is of the super-pleaser type, you will do everything within your power to please everyone. But like they say, haters are gonna hate. You simply cannot please every person. The key is to please the people that matter. Not all criticism is bad. Criticism or constructive feedback can actually enhance your improvement.

When I coach clients on improvement, I like to get a deep understanding of what they are trying to achieve and how they are going to go about it. This allows me to offer a sounding board to the changes proposed. It's a method I use to ensure that criticism converts to a feedback loop. It creates a discipline of seeking input into your proposed actions as opposed to resisting any effort to provide advice.

Fear of criticism, though, can be crippling, and in most cases is attached to a lifetime of negative issues and feelings. Often this is traced back to a past life event involving a well-hidden subconscious belief that you will always be placed under a critical microscope. This then takes significant personal coaching to correct. If you find yourself in this cycle, you should reach out to a professional trained in personal coaching techniques who can help you manage the process.

Fear of Success

Despite wanting to achieve change, some business owners self-sabotage their efforts and put every roadblock and excuse in the way to stop reaching an improved position. It's a bizarre mix… wanting something so badly, yet doing everything within your power to NOT achieve it. Much like with criticism, people who experience this will have had an experience, or series of experiences, at some stage of their life, that has stayed with them, causing this to happen. It is often a fear of detachment from the identity they have built for themselves that is at fault here. What's more, the self-sabotage is known, yet the cause hidden far away in the index of the mind. Often it is not a thing, but a concept or belief that is to blame. The most common example of this is family entanglement, where an individual feels if they move outside who they have always been within the family unit – their place, if you like – they will be banished from the flock. This occurs regularly when a person comes from a struggling family, yet resists success when it is put in front of them.

Much like with criticism, dealing with these types of issues requires working with a trained professional who can untangle the attachment that you have to family. Identification of the issue and resolution to a place where you can progress are paramount. If you are in this position, seek out a professional personal coach with experience in this area.

Case Study: The Fire-Breathing Dragon

I worked years ago with a client named Cheryl. Cheryl had a cheerful and lively personality, yet lacked confidence in all she did. She was old-fashioned, a bit of a ditherer, but that was Cheryl. Cheryl had me helping her business on an annual coaching contract, back in the days before I formulated my method as the Vector Business Platform. As part of Cheryl's Accountability session we were working on her conversion rates from quotes. Her rate had suddenly dropped off a cliff. 'Why are you not converting quotes?' I asked. Cheryl pointed me to the filing cabinet which was FULL of quotes that had not been followed up.

Now, at this point, I could quite easily have given Cheryl a script to follow, and told her to pick up the phone and get stuck in. Problem is, it would not have made any difference. After using some neuro-linguistic programming (NLP) tools and listening to her story, I found out Cheryl had lived her whole life under a shadow of criticism and rejection. It started as a child when her parents abandoned her, continued to a marriage where she was told she was constantly wrong, and now caused her to be sitting at her desk looking at a filing cabinet which may as well have been a fire-breathing dragon. She was frozen when it came to taking action, as a result of her learned or experienced behaviours.

Through some significant and confidential work, I was able to use a version of timeline therapy to bring Cheryl to a more comfortable position with customers. I gave her the tools, as well as the knowledge that the customers were more upset if she did not call than if she did. After all, they are the ones who asked for the quote in the first place.

CONSTANT IMPROVEMENT

Improvement doesn't just happen, then end. Earlier in this book I asked you to ponder the question, 'What will this business of yours look like when it is fully cooked?' Well, it turns out that business is more like cooking sourdough than a steak. If you have ever cooked sourdough, you know the artisan approach that is taken. The constant tweaking; the tending to the mother culture, which continually changes and improves. Each loaf is slightly different, even in a small way, even though you have kept everything else constant as part of your system. Maybe external factors affected the outcome.

A business is no different. It will never be fully complete. You will always be seeking to do something new. There will always be an opportunity to take or assess, a threat that has arisen that needs to be dealt with. See how this all starts to work together? Improvement is pulling all of these levers as needed. And improvement is constant. Stop improving and you will start to retrograde. This is extremely important for those who ranked as At Altitude in our Business Scorecard in Chapter 4. Keep evolving; don't take the foot off the pedal. Maintaining the business At Altitude takes just as much work as getting there. The only differences are that you have more resources at your disposal, and more varied issues. Improvement is constant.

WHAT WORKS, WHAT DOESN'T, ADJUST

To get improvement right in your business, you have to be prepared to try things. Not everything is going to go smoothly. Yet a great proportion of what you do try is going to stick. Celebrate that stuff, and the things that don't? Simply adjust until they do.

Some ideas just stink, and you have to be comfortable with that. If they really stink, move on from them quickly, learn from where they went wrong and build better solutions in the future.

Let's take a look at how to build a strong culture and structure around improvement.

Step 1: Chunk Your Tasks Down

Improvement is a game of small wins. Every task that you do is made up of many components. Just like when creating your procedures and systems, you need to bring things back to their lowest common denominator. Then look at how you can improve each facet.

Step 2: Decide How to Improve

Each improvement is like a scientific experiment. *I wonder what would happen if?* Crafted the right way this is called a hypothesis. *If I do A, I am thinking B will happen.* You then test your hypothesis by putting it into action. If it does not succeed, why? Is it able to be corrected so that it does work the way you want, or do you have to scrap the method? Or, in fact, have you proven the hypothesis wrong, in which case you need to scrap the entire thing? This hypothesis, test, correct method should be at the heart of every improvement in your business.

Step 3: Have a Sounding Board

When performing steps 1 and 2 it is a great idea to have a third party (normally a business coach or key advisor) as your sounding board. Business can be a lonely place and the tendency is to believe your own hype and not listen to feedback. Having someone who can help you break down tasks and prioritise what should be improved on is a valuable resource. A great sounding board partner will listen to your ideas and question you; however, they should not come up with ideas themselves. After all, you are wanting them to be a sounding board, not a consultant.

Step 4: Seek Out Your Team's Ideas

Just like a sounding board, your team can be a great source of feedback. The added bonus of your team's input is that they are at the coalface. They will be the ones implementing the improvements you come up with. They know what works and what currently doesn't. Who better to assist in the quest for constant improvement? Be careful though that your team does not derail the process. As mentioned previously, change is difficult and often people will seek improvements in areas that benefit them, not the organisation as a whole.

Step 5: Have Accountability and Deadlines

If you set out on a schedule of improvement over the course of the year, you need to do it in a stepped and timely fashion. To do this, it pays to have someone hold you accountable to your actions. We will cover accountability in detail in the next chapter, however you should build in a regular improvement session with your sounding board and accountability partner/s at least on a monthly basis. The meeting should run to the following agenda:

- Review of improvement projects from last meeting
- What worked, what didn't and how do we adjust?
- What new improvement projects are we seeking to start?
- Are they worthwhile improvements that we should prioritise?
- Set actions for improvement projects for before next meeting.

Case Study: All About Perspective

At times, for myself as a coach, improvement is all about being a sounding board to a business owner's ideas. The challenge is to listen and provide non-judgemental advice, yet also keep an eye out for when a business owner buys in to their own excuses.

I recently worked with a student-based business. The owner was seeking top-line growth. More students, more income equals more ability to draw a higher remuneration figure. Fitness and student-related businesses often provide a lifestyle fix for their owners. This leads to great knowledge over the things that matter in a business, and an intimate knowledge of their product.

To achieve top-line growth, we set about focusing on KPIs around leads generated, conversion to trial, conversion to student and retention of students. Turned out the problem was not with leads or even sales incoming – it was all about retention. It was like trying to fill a bath without the plug in.

From an improvement perspective, much work was required to isolate where the issues were. The owner knew it, yet needed to be constantly challenged on making assumptions based on his gut feel, or what he felt like implementing.

At our last meeting, the business had implemented structures around each age group and the reasons for their exit from the business. This granular information will form part of future class structuring and communications with parents at key times.

SUMMARY

Systems and procedures are the glue that hold an improvement project together. Improvements or changes will be short-lived if not followed or well implemented, and strong procedures and systems surrounding those changes ensure that great implementation occurs.

Managing change is a challenge, as every individual reacts in a different way. Some take change in their stride, while others have deep-seated fear, past experiences and other ingrained traits that make change extremely hard. Understanding the nuances of each person within the organisation can allow you to design procedures that alleviate much of their concerns. For everything else, get experts in to help drive the individual's performance and address any deep-seated patterns.

You will always be changing and improving something. Business will change, team members and therefore skill sets will change, economic impacts will change and personally, you will too. It's this evolution of business that has you in a constant improvement loop. It is why, within the Vector Business Platform, we devote nine months of the 12-month cycle to oscillating between Improvement and Accountability. Improvement is the engine room of business development, so if you want that awesome business and awesome life, you had better get used to it.

Once you are in the improvement loop, make sure that you implement the five-step improvement structure:

1. Chunk down tasks
2. Decide how to improve
3. Get a sounding board
4. Listen to your team's ideas
5. Create accountability and deadlines.

Improvement brings vibrancy to your business and, if built into your culture, can achieve amazing things over a period of time. Nothing happens if you just stand still.

CHAPTER 8

ACCOUNTABILITY

I don't know about you, but thinking about all this work that needs to be done to create an awesome business and awesome life, while exciting, has me needing to take a long break. Maybe I'll have a lie down and take it easy for a bit. You know, there are other things that need doing right now. I have that holiday to organise, and Mr Smith just rang with a massive complaint about his machine that broke down. I just don't think I have the time to get started yet. I might come back to things in a week or so.

Does this sound familiar?

WELL, STOP IT!

JUST

STOP!

On any given day you will have competing demands for your time and resources. You get to choose how you spend both. Sure, urgent matters jump in, but ask yourself why. There's normally an underlying reason why you can't, or choose not to, focus on what is important.

If you take anything out of this book (and I hope you take a lot more!), it needs to be the fact that you MUST have accountability to what you have said you are going to do. Now, by accountability, I don't mean someone to simply remind you. I mean someone who is going to challenge you – even treat you like a naughty child sometimes. Whatever it takes to get you to do the things you set out to do. At times, you will need the stick. Other times it's the carrot. And most of the time it's an ear to listen and a reassuring voice to keep you on track.

Accountability is one of the highest-ranked needs of small business owners, yet most don't do anything about it. So, who is going to hold you accountable?

THE CARROT AND THE STICK

My coaching style has been described as Gordon Ramsay meets Mother Theresa. Equal parts: whack 'em over the head and empathy. Fact is, depending on the circumstances, holding an individual accountable to their actions is a dark art. There are different personalities: those who accept input, and those who resist it at every turn. There are people who challenge me on what I say, which is great, as it proves they're listening. In fact, if you can get to this point with your coach, it is ideal. It will bring out the best in both of you. When the stick is needed, you will listen and adjust accordingly. When the carrot is dangled in front of you, you will pursue your goal with vigour.

When is the Stick Used?

Humans are not animals, yet I liken the stick approach to that of a thoroughbred racehorse. The average thoroughbred is a powerful beast. They can average 65 km per hour and weigh on average 450 kg. A jockey, on the other hand, weighs an average of 50 kg and is attached to the thoroughbred by their feet (the irons), their hands (the reins) and a saddle no thicker than an exercise book. Now place that horse in a group of 10, all competing for the ideal run. Jockey skill aside, there are times when the horse needs to be moved – whether that be directionally or in terms of speed. Ethics aside, the whip serves this purpose. The horse is given a series of corrective strokes and guided where it needs to go. Thing is, the horse has been trained on how to take the run. The horse has been trained to quicken when needed. At times, though, it needs that reminder, that prompt. The business owner is similar. I obviously don't use an actual whip – the term 'stick' is a metaphor for persuasion. I need to use different forms of persuasion to get movement in many instances. Take, for example, a business owner who is focusing on all the bright shiny objects and not paying attention to following up quotes or doing invoicing. A simple correction through firm accountability is needed (the stick). If your accountability partner just lets you keep going the way you are, get a new one. In this example, invoicing and quote follow-up are so fundamental to profitability and cashflow that if nothing happens the business is at severe risk of not only underperformance, but financial ruin. It often takes a wake-up call (the stick), delivered by an experienced coach or advisor, to shock things back into action.

Case Study: The Gordon Ramsay Approach

Client: Cashflow is tight. I'm too busy.

Me: What is this job board?

Client: Oh, that's where I keep track of what work is due, at each stage.

Me: Okay, so where's this one up to?

Client: Oh, I'll have to check.

Me: What about this one? Has it been invoiced?

Client: Oh, no... I need to get on to that one.

Me: [Grabs whiteboard eraser and wipes all jobs off job board].

You get the idea. The conversation that followed was quite intense. The issue was that the client was saying yes to everything, so that he didn't let people down, yet by having so much on, he was in fact disappointing more people than ever. The client admitted the session with me really shook him up. Good – it was what was needed.

What about the Carrot?

Other situations call for a motivational approach. Moving away from pain and towards pleasure is a universal truth. When faced with circumstances that demand action, the framing of the consequences of action/inaction can get real results. Let's use the same example of a business owner who is not following up quotes or producing invoices for work done. If we take the carrot approach in this example, we would quantify the financial aspects of not doing/doing the work needed. How much is the lack of invoicing costing the business? How much is the lack of follow-up affecting the sales pipeline? What would things look like and what would be possible if they did complete those tasks? This carrot approach is geared towards building enough emotion and desire into the process to elicit action.

Case Study: The Mother Theresa Approach

Not everyone responds to the stick. An accountant I was coaching had significant changes to make in terms of not only her role, but the practice as a whole. She wanted to move into a new style of work with clients, yet was not prepared to move away from the basic tasks she was doing that her staff were pleading with her to give to them. After trying the hard approach, it was clear that, as they say, you get more flies with honey. By putting in place actions around small tasks, we were able to gain traction with delegation. To me, there is still massive room for improvement. It doesn't matter what I think, though. My job is to elicit the results, which in this case, may just take a little longer, but they will come.

WHAT TO MEASURE AND HOW

Following are the most common accountability styles we work on with clients:

- **KPI monitoring:** KPI monitoring is one of the most common forms of accountability. The first element of KPI monitoring is the setting of targets for key drivers. You should then monitor your KPIs monthly in a structured manner. The key is not simply monitoring but interpreting any variances and taking ongoing corrective action, tweaking and adjusting on your way to your end goal.
- **Support from an accountant, coach or advisory board:** By enlisting your accountant/coach or an advisory board

to conduct monthly meetings, you have at your disposal a virtual CFO or executive management tier that would not otherwise be possible within your business. This allows a sounding board for ideas, a non-financial partner in your business and a key source of innovative ideas, strategies and a wealth of industry and non-industry business experience.

- **Peer coaching groups:** You can get accountability as part of a peer coaching group of like-minded executive owners, meeting regularly to share, engage and inspire. Such groups bring together significant experience as well as putting motivation into the equation through required meeting preparation and the sharing of broad category results.

If you are to be held accountable to someone, the big question you probably have is, 'What am I going to be held accountable for?' Accountability should tackle two areas:

1. Accountability for actions
2. Accountability for the key drivers and numbers (KPIs).

Actions

Part of the planning process that we discussed in Chapter 6 was chunking down your plan into 90-day sprints with specific objectives, strategies and actions. It is these actions that need to form part of your accountability structure. You should plan monthly accountability sessions throughout each sprint. These sessions should include time reviewing your actions agreed to at the last meeting against your progress. If the action hasn't been completed, why? Does the action require adjusting? Do you need to reset the priorities and timeline of the action? If the action was completed, what was the result? Do you need to do more? Your plan should not have a laundry list of actions to be completed every month. Simply list the actions from the previous month, perform the exercise above, then set, in line with your flexible plan, the actions for the next month. This is why Accountability works in tandem with Improvement. You cannot combine accountability and improvement sessions, as they each require different work. Accountability helps you focus on what needs to be done. It is not for analysing or creating new improvement tasks.

Key Performance Indicators (KPIs)

KPIs are the monitors for your business. They are a bit like medical observations: blood pressure, heart rate, blood analysis and other health data.

Each business has two types of KPIs: financial and non-financial. Financial KPIs come from a well-developed accounting system and include metrics such as gross profit margin, debtor and inventory days, trends and percentages. What you are after is an at-a-glance dashboard, either data or visually driven. Many modern software products are designed specifically for this task, although a simple spreadsheet can manage exactly the same result. With financial data, you are looking for comparison against target/budget or prior period.

When using financial KPIs, it is critical that accurate interpretation be performed. Without interpretation a number taken at face value can result in incorrect decisions being made. A basic example of this would be to review a KPI of total sales without analysing a second KPI of gross profit. More sales at a lower gross profit can actually have you in a worse position than before. KPIs are an ecosystem of measures that need to be read together.

Non-financial KPIs look at the drivers behind the numbers. It may be a conversion rate from quote or trial. It may be retention rate for, say, a gym or student-based organisation. Days in workflow could be a measure for professional services or manufacturing. Reworks, sales calls made, database growth – the sky is the limit when looking at what to measure. You should be careful though not to measure the wrong things.

The Measurement Myth

Since the 1950s, Peter Drucker's concept of 'What gets measured, gets managed' has become ingrained in our psyches. You might be surprised to know that, as subsequent articles have pointed out, Drucker never actually intended his statement to have the impact it did.

Now I don't want to get too academic, but two years after Drucker's statement, an article by VF Ridgeway set out to highlight the problems with managing a business based purely on data measurement and targets. In particular, Ridgeway raised the tendency for business managers to be solely focused on certain measurements – or KPIs, as we commonly call them – to the detriment of critical drivers.

There is a lot to take away from Ridgeway's article, but I think there is an even more fundamental issue in business at the moment. That is:

*Businesses measure TOO MANY things, and often the
WRONG things.*

Business owners now have real-time financials at their fingertips and normally a bunch of other metrics coming from various software platforms. This has the business owner in a form of analysis paralysis. What is required is FOCUS on the KEY numbers, measuring only the things that you need to manage.

I recently worked with a client who created their own spreadsheet to 'measure and manage'. With every colour of the rainbow used to highlight data and a dazzling array of charts and trends, the business owner proudly presented this as their dashboard and key to business success.

When asked what actions were being taken as a result of the analysis, they rattled off a laundry list of tasks to be achieved.

Very little was actually being achieved, though. Due to the lack of focus on key drivers of business success, the client's thoughts and strategies were scattered. Their team was confused by the endless micro approach, as well as the need to meet targets at so many different levels.

While a challenge, the client is now tasked with simplifying their approach. One page of analysis with five key numbers.

Track your Five Key Numbers

Whenever I mention having five key numbers to a business owner, I'm typically met with the question, 'Which five?' It depends on what drives your business, but it is typically a mix of core and business-specific numbers.

Core numbers should focus on gross profit (or, if it's a service business, a ratio of labour efficiency) and breakeven point (used dynamically to make spending decisions).

Business-specific numbers is where you need your most critical measurements, whether they be financial or non-financial. Examples include conversion percentage (enquiry to sale), customer retention and sales meetings held. The list is exhaustive, but you MUST choose only a few – those that, if focused on, will have the biggest impact.

I think we need to refine the concept of 'What gets measured, gets managed' to one of laser focus on a small number of relevant drivers. This will free you from data paralysis and allow you to implement improvement far easier and in the right areas.

'UNSTUCKEDNESS'

Being accountable to the numbers is one thing, but to make real progress in your business you need to be open to change. It can sometimes be hard to break from established business 'habits'. Let's take a look then at how you can build the right mindset to keep you moving.

What happens when you become stuck and just won't budge? For those who are mechanically minded, think of what happens when you force something beyond its breaking point. Like a seized bolt, it can end up snapped and then require even more drastic and costly repair work. What do you do to avoid going beyond breaking point and instead getting movement, or what I like to call 'unstuckedness'?

A number of years ago, I took part in a six-month training program in neuro-linguistic programming (NLP). During the course I found myself challenged by the often left-field approach to working with clients and their roadblocks. As a business advisor I work in absolutes, not what, at the time, I saw as parlour tricks and smoke and mirrors. The skills I learned, though, go far beyond the gloss put on them by modern-day, self-professed gurus.

The key is that we all have some sort of noise going on in our brains – something that is preventing us from moving to where we want to be. This tension, described to me as an elastic band, is at the heart of every stuck business owner's problem. No matter how hard you try to move towards your chosen goal, there is a force pulling you back the opposite way. This force has its origin in your beliefs – either those you set up for yourself along your journey, or that were instilled in you at a very early age. It's this lizard brain impact that stops your progress. As it comes from an area of your brain that you have little awareness of, you will find it hard to fight without knowing how to manage it.

A knowledge of basic NLP, or having a coach with these skills, can allow you to recognise the roadblocks, reflect on the cause and seek corrective action. A basic NLP framework looks a little like this:

- What are you wanting?
- What will having that do for you?
- What things that you value will you need to give up, to allow you to get what you want?
- What will it be like when you get what you want?

A large part of this exercise is the question, 'What is it that you value that you must give up to get what you want?' This question is aimed firmly at seeking out the subconscious values that you hold close to you. Once you can isolate these limiting beliefs that don't serve you, you can work on removing them from your belief system.

A great example of this is generating leads and prospects for your business. A hidden limiting belief may be that prospects are not going to want to speak with you. You may feel like you do not deserve clients/customers of their level and stature. Until you work to resolve the source of this belief, no matter what plans and strategies you put in place, you will continue to struggle – finding all manner of ways and reasons not to approach such people. You know that it doesn't make sense, yet your beliefs leave you in this frozen state, unable to act any differently. It's a kind of involuntary brick wall that you create for yourself.

The NLP framework allows you to recognise and appreciate that the belief exists, and by applying techniques (beyond the scope of this book), you can overcome these and become unstuck.

MANAGING YOU

Self-management is central to accountability within your business. If you can't manage yourself, how are you going to be able to manage your team, customer relationships, finances and every other area of the business? It needs to start and stop with you, and the heart of managing you is time. Using your time effectively has a ripple effect on every other facet of self-management. If you manage your time well you will be laser focused, and have a clearer perspective for decision-making as a whole. Your attention to detail will improve and all facets of doing business will run more smoothly.

So how do you achieve good time management?

You need to get used to the fact that you only have 24 hours in a day. No one, other than Dolly the sheep, has been able to be cloned. There is no silver bullet to time management. You simply just need to work smarter with the 24 hours you are given.

Inherently, we are pleasure seekers:

- We seek out what fulfils us
- We aim to please
- We love something new
- We avoid difficulty.

As a result, we find ourselves distracted regularly and focused on all the wrong things.

There are five main strategies for getting on top of time in your business. Let's take a look at them now.

1. Understand Your Drivers

The key to starting to get your time management sorted is understanding exactly what drives you.

Are you a starter or a finisher? Many of us are good at the bigger picture but not the detail. It is essential you find out what type your personality is. There are some great tools online based on industry-standard personality tests that can give insight into who you are. You will find the links to these at **direction.com.au/ awesomebookresources**.

What is your role? Many business owners wear multiple hats. This alone causes issues with efficiency. A great idea is to map it out, to see what tasks you are currently doing – you will have the chance to do this as part of the time management challenge at the end of this chapter.

Who are you accountable to? We are all inherently pleasure seekers, remember? If we are only answerable to ourselves, we tend to 'lose' time through our own bad habits. With no one to drive us, we become complacent. Come on, stop denying it… even the most focused of us have this trait.

2. Find What Works for You

Turn off from the hype generated by the thousands of people preaching time management courses and concepts… including me.

If making lists works for you… do it.

If managing your time on paper works for you better than using an app… do it.

If keeping a journal and writing gratefulness quotes works for you... do it.

You see, while we need to develop good habits, some personalities work better with different formats. The key is understanding what's available, trying some out and finding what fits.

Also, work with your body and mind rhythms. If you work best in the morning, schedule your day accordingly and take that siesta.

3. Set Deadlines and Priorities

Have you ever noticed that you always work more efficiently when you're under pressure – when a deadline is coming up, or when you are about to go on holidays? Set self-imposed due dates for tasks and stick to them.

Prioritising is also critical. Using Stephen Covey's Quadrants approach can be really useful. This plots Urgent and Important on two axes, breaking the space into four quadrants and highlighting where you should be focusing your efforts. You can download a quadrant worksheet from **direction.com.au/ awesomebookresources**.

If all of your tasks are critical (think big elephants and frogs), you simply need to focus on one at a time and communicate to key stakeholders on the others. Underpromise, overdeliver. Learn to say no to things – it's okay to do so. It's your time, not theirs.

4. Deal with Distractions

Define your role and then compare it to what your ideal role is. Put in place a plan to move from current to ideal, removing the things you should not be doing. Delegation is a great tool for time management.

How, though, do you remove the constant distractions that happen during the day? The secret to this is being consistent, and firm in taking control. Here's how to do it:

- **Park your internal distractions:** These are distractions you create yourself – the drift-offs, the daydreams, the thousands of thoughts running through your head.
  Write them down and refocus back to what you were doing. Come back to them later when you have the time, or take note of the ones that simply don't matter.
- **Inform, negotiate and action to deal with external distractions:** When someone or something interrupts you, it can throw your whole day out. When you are trying to focus on a task, let those around you know you cannot be interrupted *(inform)*.
  If you are interrupted, *negotiate* with the relevant person on when you can get back to them. Most things aren't as urgent as they are made out to be.
  When you are ready to get back to the things that interrupted you, do so, as a focused task *(action)*.
- **Stay the course when you are focused:** If you have set aside an hour to get something done, be firm and don't stop until you're finished.

5. Focus

Having laser focus is essential in mastering your time management. It ensures that tasks are completed rather than mixed with the rest of the items on your to-do list. Multitasking is the enemy of efficiency and arises when day-to-day activities are not well organised or managed. This ad-hoc approach to getting your work done also leads to stress and overwhelm, with tasks all being completed in half measures.

Laser focus is best achieved by applying the following principles:

- **Know what needs to be done:** The more clarity you have on what the task entails, the better your chances of completing it in one go.
- **Know when it needs to be done by:** Pay attention to deadlines including those you set for yourself.
- **Know how long it will take:** Be realistic about task timeframes. There are no prizes for underestimating how long a task will take, only to find you end up with a group of things all demanding attention at the last minute.
- **Block out time:** Set time aside in your schedule to pay attention to just the one task. No interruptions, no multitasking.
- **Deal with distraction:** Use the methods outlined earlier to deal with your distractions. If distracted, deal with it, then refocus back on to the task at hand.

Applying focus to your tasks will see you achieve more in your available time, and in turn creates room for more strategic thinking regarding the management of your business.

Take the Time Management Challenge

Now it's time for you to take the time management challenge. Figure 8.1 lists a set of tasks for you to complete over the next seven days. If you miss a day of the challenge you need to go back to the start. Time management will change your business monumentally. Take this challenge seriously and your business and personal lives will improve infinitely.

Figure 8.1: Time Management Challenge

YOUR ROLE

DAY 1 Review your role analysis using the Role worksheet in the Resources section of this book. Is there anything that needs to move or change? List three immediate actions based on the list and implement them.

BRAIN DUMP YOUR TO DO LIST

DAY 2 Take an A4 sheet of paper (or a spreadsheet if you want to go paperless) and list all tasks, big, small, urgent, non-urgent, important, not important. This list is a complete brain dump of everything you have going on in your head that needs action.

TRANSFER YOUR LIST INTO QUADRANTS

DAY 3 Break your to-do list into four quadrants based on how important the task is, as well as how urgent. This will help you see where your focus is going. Do you see a pattern?

ORGANISE YOUR LIST

DAY 4 Find a tool that works for you to keep track of your list. You can use a manual diary or an online project manager like Trello (a free account is all you need).

LIST OF PRIORITIES

DAY 5 Using the tool you chose on Day 4, get some commitment happening around when you will get tasks done. This is an ongoing process, so don't worry if you stumble at the first attempt.

DEAL WITH DISTRACTIONS

DAY 6 Put in place your INFORM – NEGOTIATE – ACTION rules.

POMODORO

DAY 7 Buy a manual timer (make it old-school funky like a ticking tomato) or download the iOS app Be Focused or similar. Start building a habit of using pomodoros to give you focus on your tasks. Use it as often as you wish; it doesn't have to be done every day, but consistency breeds habit.

IF YOU SKIP A DAY. STOP....

Go back to Day 1 and start again. Even if you have already done the previous steps, take time to review them and update in order. Once all seven days of the challenge have been completed, days 4 and 5 will be ongoing. All other days are the habits that surround your core list.

SUMMARY

Accountability ensures things get done in your business. It is very hard, though, to provide yourself accountability, including the carrot or stick approach. It would be a bit weird giving yourself a stern conversation on non-performance, wouldn't it?

Getting yourself a dedicated accountability partner, such as a well-qualified coach, can pay significant dividends. They can provide you with the structure and discipline needed to achieve results.

Part of that accountability structure should be having a robust KPI dashboard, so that you can measure the numbers that matter at a glance.

A great accountability partner can also help when you become stuck and simply can't break through, which often happens as a result of your own limiting beliefs. Choosing an accountability partner with a strong financial background as well as psychological skills – such as NLP/personal coaching – provides you with a diverse experience.

Lastly, no accountability will have any affect if you cannot manage yourself. Mastering time management provides the ripples throughout both your business and your personal life, allowing you to truly create the awesomeness that awaits your arrival.

PART III
ARRIVALS

*'Ladies and gentlemen, the captain has turned on the
seatbelt sign in preparation for our arrival.'*

Your head is probably by now spinning with everything
that either needs to happen or has happened within your
business.

If you are reading Part III before you have applied the
areas that make up the Vector Business Platform, make sure
that you come back and read it again in a year's time, once
the bulk of your first 12-month cycle is complete.

If you have been working through the platform steps,
one at a time, and are now towards the end of your first
12-month cycle, now is the time to reflect. You have arrived
at your first destination. What is important now is that you
take time to look back on your progress so far, and prepare
for the next leg of your journey. Business is not a 12-month
cycle in isolation. Reflect and repeat. Let's get ready to land
this thing, disembark, refuel and reboard.

CHAPTER 9

TIME TO CHECK IN

A year goes very quickly in business. If you have been applying the Vector Business Platform steps as you worked through this book, you will have been reflecting and checking in on progress along the way. However, annual resets provide a great opportunity to mentally compartmentalise your progress. Have you had a good year – in your business, and personally?

As part of checking in, you need to look behind you to see how far you have progressed. There will be both wins to celebrate and lessons to take onboard. Things that have worked and things that, while they failed, have taught you a whole lot.

It's a great time to consider what your business and personal life look like NOW. Again, you should also reflect on what they were like when you started this process. In addition, it is worth considering whether you have completed the process to your satisfaction, or if there is still plenty of work to do. (Hint: there's always more work to do.)

It is also critical that you celebrate how far you have travelled. Congratulations on arriving, but don't stop now.

REAR-VIEW MIRROR

Have you ever heard the quote by Mary Engelbreit, 'Don't look back – you're not going that way'? While I get the sentiment, ignoring where you have come from means you are ignoring both the motivating power of progress, as well as the impact of learning valuable lessons.

The rear-view mirror approach ensures that you are in fact always seeking to progress beyond where you have been.

So, what do you want to look back on? Firstly, you should look at key numbers in your business such as sales, gross profit and surplus cashflow – all areas that you should have been monitoring through your monthly KPI accountability measurements. It is also important to analyse the performance in each area and the reasons behind each result, whether positive or negative. If it is positive, how do you do more of that? If it is negative, can you do things differently?

Secondly, you should look back on the objectives you set yourself in the Awareness stage, as well as your business action plan. Which of the things that you originally set out to do have you actually achieved? If you haven't achieved some of your intended goals, why not?

Your rear-view mirror should also spill over into your personal life. Remember, you are trying to create an awesome business AND an awesome life and the integration of the two creates your overall achievement level. Look back on the areas where you were wanting to see change in your personal life. Was it time with family, purchase of a major asset, reduction of debt or more travel? Achieving your personal goals is just as important as achieving your business goals.

As you move from the end of your 12-month cycle to the start of your next, you will once again perform a business valuation.

As you will recall from Chapter 3, business value is a factor of risk and profitability. Looking back on how risk has evolved in your business, as well as any profit improvement, allows you to see your business asset's capital growth.

WINS AND LESSONS

Now that you have looked back at your progress over the last 12 months, what wins should you recognise? Recognising your achievements provides motivation and drive to continue your business development. When recognising your wins, it is important that you recognise not only the big noticeable wins, but also the small, almost insignificant successes that have occurred.

Let's go back to your original Vector Business Scorecard, which you completed in Chapter 4. In what areas did you originally rank low? Without taking the scorecard again, think about the progress you have made over the last 12 months in these areas. Have you increased sales, gained customers, improved profitability, added team members, acquired assets, taken up opportunities, perhaps even won an award? Stop for a moment and think about those wins, big or small, that you have achieved.

Let's be real, though: not everything would have been sunshine and lollipops during the year. What are the things that went wrong, and what lessons did you take from the process? These lessons are important, as they are either things that you will recast into the next 12 months or move away from, knowing that you fired your best shot and they just didn't work.

What are the key insights that the last year has given you – not only in your business, but also yourself? This exercise is not about being exact, but about recognising those things that you may have forgotten along the way. You will have made more progress than you think – now is the time to take that progress and do something with it. The hard work has been done; you have started the momentum. Don't stop now.

YOUR BUSINESS LIFE NOW

It's time to take a moment to break down what your business life looks like now. To assist you in this process let's check in on your progress in each of the five Vector Business Platform disciplines.

Awareness

Of the needs you outlined at the start of the year, which do you feel have been addressed effectively? Have any needs been unmet? Take note of any unmet needs for your reset exercise in Chapter 10.

In terms of business value, what areas of risk have you been able to improve on? Have you made your business more attractive to a potential buyer in the last 12 months? Has profitability improved and, if so, what effect do you believe this has had in terms of the value of your business?

Has your desired magic number for your future changed? If it has, has it increased or decreased?

What effect did targeting your quick wins through hidden profits analysis have on your business over the last 12 months?

Numbers

You should by now have a source of reliable financial data coming from your internal systems. To ensure that you are ready for the next stage in your business growth, how comfortable are you in your ability to interpret your numbers? Have your numbers improved, and if they have, do you understand what has contributed to that growth? What areas of understanding your financials do you now need to work on to master them? Did you reach budget in terms of your business money plan?

Planning

How much of your business action plan was implemented? It's okay to not have completed it all. We work in a realistic environment here. Yet it's important to note any unfinished plans you have before you go about making even more. What could make implementation of the plan easier in the year ahead?

Improvement

What are your top three improvement successes for the year? Have you managed to finish the year with standard operating procedures documented in an online document management system or on an intranet? What worked, what didn't and what now needs adjusting?

Accountability

Where did the going get tough for you? What have been your top three struggles, and did you overcome them? If you could go back, what would you do differently? Is this relevant to you going forward? If you are honest with yourself, how would you rank your effort individually this year out of 10, and where could you improve?

YOUR PERSONAL LIFE NOW

I want to revisit the work/life integration concept again at this important stage. It is critical that you check in on what your personal life is like NOW. Remember that you set out on this journey we call business for a number of different reasons, and one of those was most likely to do with flexibility in your personal life. There was most likely a thought of personal wealth creation in there as well.

So how have you gone in achieving results in your personal life, away from the business? Have you been able to create separate time to enjoy life outside of work, or has the business been all-consuming? No matter what your answer is, the next 12 months will not be, and does not need to be, the same as the last. This is because, as previously covered, there is no balance – there will always be extremes in both your personal and business lives. The essential part is to improve your position in each: creating a thriving business and an awesome personal life.

Time for a personal check-in quiz – give yourself a score out of five for each item (one being a big fat NO and five being a resounding YES).

Are you:	Score (1–5)
Spending enough time with those most important to you?	
Able to enjoy spending time on personal hobbies or pursuits?	
Able to maintain a healthy lifestyle?	
Creating wealth outside of your business?	
Able to contribute to the community or world at large, making an impact that surpasses both your business and personal lives?	
Total score (out of 25)	

Scoring:

- **17 or higher:** You are killing it. Keep it up.
- **10–17:** Keep going, you are building momentum. Try making small improvements to each area now.
- **Below 10:** Don't get disheartened, change takes time. Choose just one area to improve for now.

All of these areas add to an awesome life; however, you need to do YOU. Whatever creates your awesomeness, just make sure you are achieving that.

CELEBRATING SUCCESS

Everyone loves a celebration, right? Well, now is the time to plan yours. If you have a team, involve them. If it's just you, still celebrate. One rule though: make it special. You didn't come this far to just move on to the next year with no fanfare, did you? I know the effort you have put in – hell, I wish I could come and celebrate with you (my email for the invite is in the back of the book ☺).

Too often, we deny ourselves the celebration of our own achievements. Many of us were brought up to be humble, to not put ourselves out there for fear of tall poppy syndrome. However, now is your time, so it's time to celebrate. And while the ultimate choice is yours, here are some basic parameters:

- Spend the equivalent of 50% of each individual's weekly wage as a budget.
- Make the activity all inclusive – if some members of the team aren't keen on jumping out of a plane, don't go skydiving.
- Create an experience. The budget is not about the money, it's to enable the experience.

You see, it's the ability to celebrate, and realise what we are actually celebrating, that makes the difference here. It is less about the quantum of the gift and more about the feeling of *WOW... this is what happens when everything clicks.* Remember that pain you wanted to move away from? This is the pleasure you want to move towards. The feeling that you have accomplished what you set out to do. Don't let that go unrewarded.

SUMMARY

Now that you have reconsidered the five Vector Business Model disciplines in more detail, how do you feel about your business journey over the last 12 months? I guarantee that you will either have made progress or made an excuse. Simply put: the process, when followed, elicits action. Those actions, when well directed, create progress. That is what being a Vector Business is all about: direction with magnitude. These two together, when well-aimed, create significant impact on your personal and business lives.

I'd now like you to retake the Vector Business Scorecard. Be honest with your assessments. Remember that the bands may have you at the same level for a number of years despite making great progress. It's the interpretation of the answers that is most important. As part of completing the scorecard, you receive a free half-hour coaching session to review and discuss your results. This half-hour is the glue that holds it all together, so take advantage of it.

To access your scorecard go to: **direction.com.au/vector businessscore**.

CHAPTER 10

BRINGING IT ALL TOGETHER

By now you will have celebrated your wins and your achievements so far. Now it's time to make sure that the circle on your first 12-month process is closed.

The evolution of your business will continue for as long as you own it, as will the evolution of your personal life. This evolution, though, is a continuous loop. Where are you now? What do you want to achieve? How are you going to achieve it? By resetting after each 12-month journey, you can prepare once again for departure on your next 12 months.

Throughout this book we have been focused on you and your business. However, a final important check-in needs to be done with your customers. Their feedback can ensure that you are aiming correctly with your business. After all, while we want a business to be on our terms, ultimately it is our customers' willingness to buy from us that makes everything work. Their feedback is therefore vital as you plan your next steps. It's a final step in bringing the Vector Business Platform together.

After considering your client feedback, you are left with your final decision: where are you heading now? It's time to reset for the next destination – and that will lead you back to the start of the Vector Business Platform and indeed the start of this book.

THE CONTINUOUS LOOP

A lot of people ask me, 'How long should I work with a business coach or advisor?' My answer is always: continually. Remember this: staying stationary is not an option. In this fast-paced economy, what you did last year is already being surpassed by your competition. Customers and clients are increasingly demanding and have a wealth of information – and, as a result, a world of choice – at their disposal. This means that if you stop evolving and adjusting, you will start going backwards. You are probably getting sick of hearing that fact, but ignore it at your peril.

My recommended process is this: at the end of every 12 months, assess your progress, exactly the way we did in the previous chapter. This gives you the opportunity to reflect on where you have come from and where you want to go. Once you have assessed your progress and determined the next destination, the question is, what process will you use to get there? I am hoping that the Vector Business Platform has shown you that putting a structured process around your business and individual needs can help you achieve remarkable things.

Then, as you reset for the next run through the 12-month loop, ensure that any unfinished business is evaluated and carried forward to the next 12 months if relevant.

By continuing with your development, you will ride the high with your team as well. You have just come off celebrating your wins from last year. To revert back to business as usual is to flatten the enthusiasm you have built. The positive belief system that you have built in your team is now ready to harvest. Do not walk away; lean in.

CLIENT FEEDBACK

Your customers want to buy from you. They want to be loyal. However, if you do not provide a solution to their problems they will be forced to look for an alternative. Do not allow them this ability. The key to this is to seek client feedback. You can adopt methods such as Net Promoter Score and all other manners of measurements, but at the end of the day, what you are interested in is two things:

1. **Are there any services you do NOT provide that your customers are seeking?** This simple question can glean strategies and objectives that you simply may have not uncovered otherwise. It can also help you avoid heading down avenues that have no relevance to your customers, let alone prospects. Ask the question and evaluate the feedback. Obviously, you are not going to act on every request a client has, as there must be a business case for every opportunity. Becoming aware of their thoughts, however, is essential.
2. **Where can your service improve?** It's sometimes not about the product but about the overall buying experience. You can have the greatest product under the sun, however the pricing may be wrong, the service may be terrible, or the after-sales experience a turn-off. Getting all of these factors in sync will drive customer loyalty.

Choosing the format to get client feedback will depend on the style of your business. If you work heavily one-on-one, such as in a service business, then face-to-face or by phone may work well. If you need to scale the process, given your high volume of customers, maybe email or online survey tools may be more appropriate.

Whatever the method, ask the questions and absorb the feedback. Incorporate that feedback into your future plans. This will allow a very focused strategic plan to be created in line with customer needs, not just your assumptions.

WHERE ARE YOU HEADING?

Okay. Time to make the call on where you are heading next. By the time you have reached this section you have checked in on your business and personal progress over the last 12 months. You have considered your progress in each of the five disciplines of the Vector Business Platform and gained feedback from your customers. The ball is now in your court as to where you want to take this business next. To determine that, let's go right back to the beginning. What will your business look like when it is fully cooked?

If you performed that original exercise correctly, you will have set some longer targets that were clearly not achievable within the first 12 months. You would have recognised, then, that this is not a short-term project. It will span many years. You will also move the goalposts slightly as your ultimate destination gets closer.

I often use a timeline with clients when we get to this point. Much of the initial grind has been cleared and now we can look at the timing of business development in the knowledge that things CAN happen.

Look at your end point again. Has it changed? Have you surpassed where you were expecting to be at the start of the year, or are you sticking to the course originally plotted? Once the end destination is set, let's mark on the left-hand side of the timeline where you are now.

Take a look at your timeline. How many years do you think are between now and the future point? Simply divide your plan up and you will start to see how many years you are away from achieving your target. This will be the basis for your next year of planning.

This process is slightly different from the first year. The reason for this is that the first year was focused on getting the building blocks in place. When you started, did you have a business value on hand, a business action plan formulated or KPI systems in place? Now that you have built these once, you can revise them infinitely. Will they change? You bet. However, you now understand the concept and the development. You will find the strategy and implementation of year two onwards is just as challenging as building the blocks from the start.

SUMMARY

We have covered a lot of ground to get to this point. Many building blocks have now been learned and put in place for the future. Once again, though, don't stop now. Building your business and achieving what you originally set out to do simply doesn't happen in the space of one year. And if it does, I guarantee your future goals will have to be refined and reset.

This continuous loop is essential for results as well as keeping momentum in the process.

Taking on client feedback at this point helps ensure that your future direction is on track in line with client needs and demands.

By taking stock of the timeline to achieve your ultimate goals, you are able to put boundaries around the next plan that you will embark on. Compartmentalising the last year and bringing it all together for next year's targets allows momentum to be maintained. By taking the time to chunk this down, you will create the clarity of knowing exactly where you need to get to in the next stage of your development.

CONCLUSION

An awesome business and an awesome life are individually unique concepts. What represents success to one person is different to another. Fundamental to the concept, though, is the ability to have your business enable what you wish to achieve in your personal life. To be an enabler, a business needs to create an income, as well as grow in value as an asset – most likely the second-largest asset you have.

The integration between your business and personal life will never be perfectly balanced. There will be times when you need to put all your attention on your business, to the detriment of time with family or even your mental wellbeing. Smart business management will see you arrive at a point where you can get more personal time and satisfaction. Beware, though: the tendency to move closer towards this side – too much light and not enough dark – can be equally bad.

To design a business that can enable the impact you wish to have, it is essential to have a structured process. This structure prevents you from jumping on the business-owner hamster wheel and not being able to get off until it's too late – and you're looking back on the years spent just grinding away.

Throughout this book, I have introduced you to the Vector Business Platform – the structured approach that I have created to use with my Inner Circle of coaching clients, helping them to achieve awesome businesses and awesome lives. The Vector Business Platform takes you through the five disciplines that we've reviewed together in this book:

- Awareness
- Numbers
- Planning
- Improvement
- Accountability.

Each of these five disciplines is broken down into key activities that, when followed, allow you to focus on your specific needs, yet also adopt a consistent approach. The tools used in applying the Vector Business Platform are implemented over a 12-month period, preferably in conjunction with a dedicated business coach. At the end of your 12 months, you will reflect on your lessons learned as well as your wins, large or small – and celebrate these with gusto.

Using the continuous loop concept, at the end of each 12-month cycle you reassess your business and personal life, as well as the progress you have made, and reset for the next 12 months of development. 'Don't stop now' is the term I use – if you remain stationary, or stop the process because you think you 'know how to do it', you will find you eventually revert to previous habits and your progress again stalls.

It is the interaction between your specific business skills, and a great accountant and coach, that will create the perfect environment for your success. As an advisor, I don't claim to be the reason for a business owner's success. It is the business owner who is solely responsible for that. My skills, and those of my team, simply provide the spine to the process – the support and guidance, the tissues for the tears, the champagne for the celebration.

At the end of this book, I have included a special invitation for your Vector Business Platform journey if you want to partner with us to ensure your success. It is your invitation only, and our thank you for coming this far.

You now have your future in your hands. You also have this book in your hands. The two are as much integrated as an awesome business and an awesome life. Use this book as your guide and your awesome future will follow.

REFERENCES

Commonwealth of Australia 2020, *Small Business Counts December 2020*, Australian Small Business and Family Enterprise Ombudsman, asbfeo.gov.au/sites/default/files/ASBFEO%20 Small%20Business%20Counts%20Dec%202020%20v2.pdf.

Tony Alessandra 1988, *Selling by Objectives*, Prentice-Hall.

The Abraham Group, Inc n.d., 'Three ways to grow your business', abraham.com/topic/three-ways-to-grow-your-business.

RSM Australia 2016, *thinkBIG 2016*, rsm.global/australia/sites/default/files/media/publications/thinkBIG/thinkbig-2016.pdf.

Australian Government, Australian Accounting Standards Board, aasb.gov.au.

Andrew Burke, Stuart Fraser and Francis J Greene 2010, 'The multiple effects of business planning on new venture performance', *Journal of Management Studies*, 47(3), 391–415.

VF Ridgway 1956, 'Dysfunctional Consequences of Performance Measurements', *Administrative Science Quarterly*, 1(2), 240–247

RESOURCES

You will find a full list of downloadable resources to accompany this book at: **direction.com.au/awesomebookresources**. Resources include:

- Pricing charts showing the effect of discounting and/or increasing prices
- Business structure comparison chart
- Business money plan template
- Automation stocktake template
- 90-day plan template
- Procedure template
- Time management challenge
- Role worksheet
- Quadrant template.

The **Vector Business Scorecard** can be accessed at: **direction.com.au/vectorbusinessscore**.

Some useful personality tests:

- **Jung Personality Test (similar to Myers-Briggs):** 123test.com/jung-personality-test
- **IMA – A colour-based personality grouping:** imahigh.com
- **Wealth Dynamics – A paid, thorough test for entrepreneurs:** wealthdynamics.geniusu.com.

ACKNOWLEDGEMENTS

It's easy to underestimate the amount of effort that goes in to bringing a book into reality. After all, the content within these pages is based on my 20-plus years of working with small business owners.

That's probably a great place to start, then. To all the business owners that I have in some way helped in their journey, I feel you are the real heroes. The endless hours, risk and get-back-up-off-the-canvas attitude that you have shown is the essence of creating an awesome business and awesome life, and a huge influence on this book.

To my massively supportive fiancée and life partner Brenda, thank you for listening to my endless work-related anecdotes. You can have me back now.

Kids – well, all in their 20s now – are essential to keep you grounded. Lara, Maddy and Josh, thank you for ensuring I never take myself too seriously.

A massive thank you to the Direction team, 'Team Awesome', who have contributed directly and indirectly to seeing me reach the finish line with this project.

A big shout out to Glen Carlson, the Dent Global team and fellow KPIs along the way who took someone who had always planned a book and gave me the clarity to be someone who actually has. Also, Lucy McCarraher and the Rethink Press team, for taking me through the writing process and teaching me many a trick along the way.

Thank you to Damon O'Shea, Suzy Spicer, Sam Benson and my brother, Terry Ross, for generously offering their time to read the book cover to cover and provide honest and constructive feedback. You helped me polish what came out of my head into something the broader market would engage with.

And of course the massive efforts of the Publish Central team for helping me deliver this polished product.

THE AUTHOR

David Ross is the director and founder of Direction Accounting and Business Coaching. He specialises in ensuring small business owners achieve the things they originally went into business for, before the white noise and chaos took over.

Over the last 20 years, David has worked with more than 1200 businesses, with his Inner Circle of clients growing by an average of 32%. This has been achieved by providing a unique blend of accounting and financial knowledge with the more nuanced, personal skills of coaching.

Often referred to as the supercoach of the accounting and business coaching industry, David excels in taking the daunting concepts of business management and converting them into easy-to-understand and practical concepts for business owners.

David lives on the coast of New South Wales, and works regularly with businesses Australia wide. In recent years, David has been instrumental in the creation of the not-for-profit organisation OK for Business, which aims to be a conduit between small business owners, mental health resources and organisations, and financial advisory services. Business is often made too hard, and David is hellbent on eliminating the negative impact running a small business has on its owners' lives and mental wellbeing.

David is the host of the 'Every Business needs a Hero' podcast and regularly appears as a speaker, podcast guest, media commentator and writer in the small business, business growth and taxation space.

When not busy working with business owners, David can be found fronting an Australian rock covers band. And who said accountants were boring!

david@direction.com.au
direction.com.au
linkedin.com/in/davidrosssupercoach

YOUR EXCLUSIVE
INVITATION TO BECOME
A VECTOR BUSINESS

By now, you will have realised that implementation and accountability are essential to achieving what you want in your business and your life. With that in mind, I would like to invite you to become part of the Inner Circle of business owners I personally work with each year, to put in place the ideas contained in this book and become a Vector Business.

As part of a select group of business owners, you will be provided with tailored support and guidance to ensure things get done, and that an awesome business and awesome life becomes a reality for you.

The Inner Circle is an exclusive offering that extends well beyond our standard services. To make sure I meet my commitment to you, places are limited to 20 businesses annually.

They say that when the student is ready, the teacher will come. If you are ready to become part of the Inner Circle simply email me at **innercircle@direction.com.au** and let me know a little more about your business journey to date.

It's all about giving you MORE DIRECTION | MORE SPEED | MORE IMPACT.